CAMBRIDGE LIBRARY COLLECTION

Books of enduring scholarly value

Cambridge

The city of Cambridge received its royal charter in 1201, having already been home to Britons, Romans and Anglo-Saxons for many centuries. Cambridge University was founded soon afterwards and celebrates its octocentenary in 2009. This series explores the history and influence of Cambridge as a centre of science, learning, and discovery, its contributions to national and global politics and culture, and its inevitable controversies and scandals.

Bibliotheca Pepysiana

Samuel Pepys (1633-1703) was a student of Magdalene College, Cambridge, and bequeathed his personal library of 3000 volumes to the College on condition that the contents remained intact and unaltered; they remain there, in his original bookcases, to this day. In the early twentieth century, a project to produce a complete catalogue was begun, and four volumes were published between 1914 and 1940. Volume 4 describes the books about shorthand which Pepys – an enthusiastic practitioner himself - methodically collected, and had bound in five volumes. Over the centuries, various specialists had consulted this important collection but this catalogue brought it to the attention of bibliographers for the first time. It provides background information about the author of each work, places the content in its historical context and supplies bibliographic details together with notes about other surviving copies. It is a valuable resource for historians of stenography and its uses.

Cambridge University Press has long been a pioneer in the reissuing of out-of-print titles from its own backlist, producing digital reprints of books that are still sought after by scholars and students but could not be reprinted economically using traditional technology. The Cambridge Library Collection extends this activity to a wider range of books which are still of importance to researchers and professionals, either for the source material they contain, or as landmarks in the history of their academic discipline.

Drawing from the world-renowned collections in the Cambridge University Library, and guided by the advice of experts in each subject area, Cambridge University Press is using state-of-the-art scanning machines in its own Printing House to capture the content of each book selected for inclusion. The files are processed to give a consistently clear, crisp image, and the books finished to the high quality standard for which the Press is recognised around the world. The latest print-on-demand technology ensures that the books will remain available indefinitely, and that orders for single or multiple copies can quickly be supplied.

The Cambridge Library Collection will bring back to life books of enduring scholarly value across a wide range of disciplines in the humanities and social sciences and in science and technology.

Bibliotheca Pepysiana

*A Descriptive Catalogue of the Library of
Samuel Pepys*

VOLUME 4: SHORTHAND BOOKS

WILLIAM JOHN CARLTON

CAMBRIDGE
UNIVERSITY PRESS

CAMBRIDGE UNIVERSITY PRESS

Cambridge New York Melbourne Madrid Cape Town Singapore São Paolo Delhi

Published in the United States of America by Cambridge University Press, New York

www.cambridge.org
Information on this title: www.cambridge.org/9781108002066

This edition first published 1940
This digitally printed version 2009

ISBN 978-1-108-00206-6

BIBLIOTHECA PEPYSIANA

Part IV. SHORTHAND BOOKS

BIBLIOTHECA PEPYSIANA

A DESCRIPTIVE CATALOGUE OF THE LIBRARY OF SAMUEL PEPYS

PART IV. SHORTHAND BOOKS

With Biographical and Bibliographical Notes

By WILLIAM J. CARLTON

LONDON

SIDGWICK & JACKSON, LTD.

MCMXL

FIRST PUBLISHED MCMXL
MADE AND PRINTED IN GREAT BRITAIN
AT THE UNIVERSITY PRESS, CAMBRIDGE
ALL RIGHTS RESERVED

LIST OF ABBREVIATIONS

Arber's Transcript = A Transcript of the Registers of the Company of Stationers of London, 1554–1640. Edited by Edward Arber, F.S.A. Vols. i–v. London, 1875–1894.

D.N.B. = Dictionary of National Biography.

Johnson = A Catalogue of Engraved and Etched English Title-pages, down to the death of William Faithorne, 1691. Compiled by Alfred Forbes Johnson. London, The Bibliographical Society, 1934.

McKerrow, Devices = Printers' and Publishers' Devices in England and Scotland, 1485–1640. By R. B. McKerrow. London, The Bibliographical Society, 1913.

McKerrow, 1557–1640 = A Dictionary of Printers and Booksellers in England, Scotland and Ireland from 1557–1640. London, The Bibliographical Society, 1910.

Plomer, 1641–1667 = A Dictionary of the Booksellers and Printers in England, Scotland and Ireland from 1641 to 1667. By Henry R. Plomer. London, The Bibliographical Society, 1907.

Plomer, 1668–1725 = A Dictionary, etc. from 1668 to 1725. By H. R. Plomer and others. Edited by A. Esdaile. London, The Bibliographical Society, 1922.

Roxb. Transcript = A Transcript of the Registers of the Worshipful Company of Stationers, from 1640–1708. Vols. i–iii. London, 1913–1914. (Transcribed by H. R. Plomer and edited by George Edward Briscoe Eyre for the Roxburghe Club.)

S.T.C. = A Short-Title Catalogue of Books printed in England, Scotland and Ireland and of English Books printed Abroad, 1475–1640. Compiled by A. W. Pollard and G. R. Redgrave. London, 1926.

T.C. = The Term Catalogues, 1668–1709, with a number for Easter Term, 1711. Edited by Prof. Edward Arber, F.S.A. Vols i–iii. London, 1903–1906.

B.G.P. = Bibliothèque Ste.-Geneviève, Paris.
B.L.M. = Bayerische Landesanstalt für Kurzschrift, Munich.
B.L.O. = Bodleian Library, Oxford.
B.M.L. = British Museum Library, London.
B.N.P. = Bibliothèque Nationale, Paris.
C.C.O. = Corpus Christi College, Oxford.
C.E.B. = C. E. Bieller-Gindrat's Library, Bienne.
C.L.E. = City Library, Exeter.
C.L.M. = Chetham Library, Manchester.
C.L.W. = Earl of Crawford's Library, Haigh Hall, Wigan.
F.L.W. = Folger Shakespeare Library, Washington, D.C.
G.L.L. = Guildhall Library, London.
I.S.W. = Institute of Shorthand Writers, London.
J.R.G. = John Robert Gregg's Library, New York City.
L.C.W. = Library of Congress, Washington, D.C.
L.N.Y. = Public Library, New York.
L.P.L. = Lambeth Palace Library, London.
M.L.W. = Warrington Museum and Library.
N.L.S. = National Library of Scotland, Edinburgh.
P.L.L. = Sir Isaac Pitman and Sons, Ltd., London.

P.L.S. = Public Library, Salem, Mass.
R.L.M. = Free Reference Library, Manchester.
S.L.D. = Sächsisches Stenographisches Landesamt, Dresden.
U.L.C. = University Library, Cambridge.
U.L.Y. = Yale University Library, New Haven, Conn.
W.J.C. = William J. Carlton's Library, Geneva.

Bailey coll. = Collection formed by John Eglington Bailey, F.S.A., Stretford, presented to R.L.M. by Councillor H. Boddington in 1889.

Beale coll. = Collection formed by Charles Currier Beale, Boston, Mass., acquired by the National Shorthand Reporters' Association, deposited in L.N.Y.

Blair coll. = Collection formed by William Blair, M.D., sold at Evans's auction rooms, London, 11 February 1823.

Byrom coll. = Collection formed by John Byrom, F.R.S., presented to C.L.M.

Cummings coll. = Collection formed by Herbert Cummings, acquired by the Library of the American Antiquarian Society, Worcester, Mass.

Fraser coll. = Collection formed by Alexander Fraser.

Guénin coll. = Collection formed by Louis Prosper Guénin, Paris, presented to B.G.P. by his son, Eugène Guénin in 1919.

Hanbury coll. = Collection formed by Benjamin Hanbury, Brixton, sold at Puttick and Simpson's auction rooms, London, 1864, acquired by L.C.W.

Harland coll. = Collection formed by John Harland, Manchester, presented to C.L.M.

Havette coll. = Collection formed by René Havette, Paris, acquired by C.E.B. in 1936.

Healey coll. = Collection formed by Horace Grant Healey, acquired by U.L.Y. in 1938.

Howard coll. = Collection formed by Jerome Bird Howard, Cincinnati, Ohio, acquired by the National Shorthand Reporters' Association, deposited in L.N.Y.

Lewis coll. = Collection formed by James Henry Lewis, dispersed in 1871–2 and mainly acquired by B.L.O., B.M.L., Birmingham Free Library and Cornelius Walford.

O'Donnell coll. = Collection formed by John O'Donnell, Manchester, partly acquired by P.L.L. and W.J.C.

O'Keefe coll. = Collection formed by David H. O'Keefe, acquired by the National Shorthand Reporters' Association, deposited in L.N.Y.

Paterson coll. = Collection formed by Alexander Paterson, Barnsley, presented to P.L.S. by William Gover in 1906.

Pocknell coll. = Collection formed by Edward Pocknell, presented to C.L.E. in 1894.

Rockwell coll. = Collection formed by Julius Ensign Rockwell, Washington, D.C., acquired by the National Shorthand Reporters' Association, deposited in L.N.Y.

Taylor coll. = Collection formed by James William Taylor, Tooting, acquired by P.L.L. in 1937.

Todd coll. = Collection formed by Robert Todd, Hadley Green, Barnet, acquired by J.R.G. and W.J.C.

Walford coll. = Collection formed by Cornelius Walford, F.S.S., acquired by C.L.W.

Warden coll. = Collection formed by John Maben Warden, Edinburgh, presented to N.L.S. in 1927.

INTRODUCTION[1]

If there is one of Samuel Pepys's many accomplishments for which posterity has reason to be particularly grateful, it is surely his knowledge of shorthand. With the exception of proper names and an occasional jumble of letters and languages (to which Pepys resorted for some of the more scandalous passages), the diary is written throughout in stenographic characters, and some of its most attractive qualities must be attributed to his proficiency in an art which, by enabling him to set down the details of many an episode before they faded from his memory, contributed to that racy spontaneity which is its greatest charm. Indeed, it is hardly too much to say that but for shorthand the diary as we know it could never have been written.

At least a score of different shorthand systems had been published in England before Pepys began to pen his famous self-revelation on 1 January 1660, three or four of them were at that time widely known and practised, and their adepts were so numerous as to excite the wonder and admiration of visitors from abroad. Perhaps the most popular of all these systems was that expounded in Thomas Shelton's *Tachygraphy*, first printed in 1635 at the Cambridge University Press. It was an improvement on an earlier presentation of the system which Shelton had launched nine years before, and at once achieved a great vogue. The title-page states that the work was "approoued by both Vnyuersities", and a former owner of one of the copies in my possession has added in MS. "espesially by Cambridge". Whatever the precise significance of this claim, there is good reason to believe that it was during his period of residence at Cambridge that Pepys acquired the rudiments of the art. Many graduates had mastered its intricacies when he went up to the university in 1651 as a youth of seventeen. Some of them had even contributed encomiastic verses to Shelton's manual, pride of place being given to some rather halting lines addressed "To the Authour his Friend" by Edward Rainbowe, who was master of Pepys's own college from 1642 to 1650.

In his *Tutor to Tachygraphy*, a companion to the textbook in the form of question and answer, Shelton enumerated some of the advantages of his short-

[1] Reprinted, with modifications, from "Samuel Pepys his Shorthand Books" (*The Library*, June, 1933).

vii

hand, among them being "secrecy, brevity, celerity and perpetuity". "Sometimes", he added, "a man may have occasion to write that which he would not have everyone acquainted with, which being set downe in these Characters, hee may have them for his owne private use onely. And I have taught diverse, who have learned it for that very end." Although the secrecy which the author claimed for his method was only relative and its deficiencies as an instrument for verbatim reporting not a few, it was well adapted for such a purpose as the keeping of a diary.

Whatever the reasons for his choice, it was Shelton's tachygraphy which Pepys studied and of which he became a skilled practitioner. Not only did he record in shorthand the events of each day for nearly ten years, but he used the art in drafting his public and private letters, and although forced to close the diary in 1669, on account of failing sight, he continued its use throughout his life. Allusions to shorthand are scattered throughout the diary. On 16 April 1661 Pepys records that he "found Mr (afterwards Sir William) Coventry reading of the Psalms in short hand (which he is now busy about), and had good sport about the long marks that are made there for sentences in divinity which he is never like to make use of".[1] After four years and a half the constant writing of shorthand made his eyes "ache ready to drop out" (8 June 1664). Pepys's use of the art in affairs of State is illustrated by the entry on 17 November 1666: "It was a great convenience tonight that what I had writ foule in short hand, I could read to W. Hewer, and he take it fair in short hand, so as I can read it tomorrow to Sir W. Coventry, and then come home, and Hewer read it to me while I take it in long hand to present, which saves me much time." On 31 July 1668 Pepys was with William Ashburnham, the King's Cofferer, "and I made him admire my drawing a thing presently [i.e., writing swiftly] in short hand; but, God knows, I have paid dear for it in my eyes". Finally, on 31 May 1669 there is the poignant last entry: "And thus ends all that I doubt I shall ever be able to do with my own eyes in the keeping of my Journall, I being not able to do it any longer, having done now so long as to undo my eyes almost every time that I take a pen in my hand; and, therefore, whatever

---

[1] Sternhold and Hopkins's metrical version of the Psalms, engraved by Thomas Cross in the shorthand system of Jeremiah Rich, was printed about this time in a very small volume, with a portrait of Rich as frontispiece (see p. 60). A similar volume, engraved by Cross in Shelton's shorthand, with a portrait of Shelton, was issued subsequently. The one which Pepys treated with such levity was probably Rich's, and the diary entry helps to fix its date.

comes of it, I must forbear; and, therefore, resolve, from this time forward, to have it kept by my people in long hand, and must be contented to set down no more than is fit for them and all the world to know; or, if there be any thing, which cannot be much, now my amours to Deb are past, and my eyes hindering me in almost all other pleasures, I must endeavour to keep a margin in my book open, to add, here and there, a note in short hand with my own hand. And so I betake myself to that course, which is almost as much as to see myself go into my grave: for which, and all the discomforts that will accompany my being blind, the good God prepare me!"

But Pepys did not lose his sight, and according to Sir D'Arcy Power his fear of becoming blind was wholly unfounded.[1] In later years his shorthand skill stood him in good stead on many occasions. In 1677, while sitting in the House as Member for Castle Rising, he took "Parliament notes" in shorthand, and marked them "To be transcribed in longhand".[2] In October 1680 he was in attendance on Charles II at Newmarket for ten days, and took down from the king's dictation the romantic story of his escape after the battle of Worcester. The original shorthand MS., endorsed "A Journall of yᵉ King's Escape from Worcester, taken by mee this day in Short-hand from yᵉ King's owne Mouth", with Pepys's signature and the date 3 October 1680, is preserved in the Pepysian Library. A longhand transcript and other relevant documents are bound up in the same volume.

A volume of Pepys's correspondence, chiefly on questions relating to the Navy, now in the National Maritime Museum at Greenwich, includes forty-five letters written in shorthand, eleven others being partly in shorthand and partly in longhand, between 1664 and 1669. They were transcribed by Mr Edwin Chappell and printed in his *Shorthand Letters of Samuel Pepys*, 1933. Short-hand copies of letters written by Pepys to his nephew John Jackson, to James Houblon (son of Pepys's old friend Sir James Houblon), and to Mrs Vernon (wife of Sir James Vernon) were among the Pepys Cockerell relics sold by auction in April 1931. Other shorthand MSS. in Pepys's autograph are in the British Museum, Bodleian Library and the Public Record Office.

In 1683 the diarist accompanied Lord Dartmouth to Tangier, and on the occasion of this visit, his subsequent travels in Spain and his return to Tangier

---

[1] "An Address on Why Samuel Pepys discontinued his Diary" (*The Lancet*, 24 June 1911).
[2] Rawlinson MS. C. 859 (Bodleian).

in 1684, he kept a second diary in shorthand which now forms part of the
Rawlinson MSS. in the Bodleian. It is, according to the late Dr Tanner, "a dull
and pedestrian record of daily happenings, only rarely illuminated by the pene-
trating observations and criticisms which the Diary so freely dispenses".
Deciphered in 1826 by the Rev. John Smith, it was first printed in the *Life,
Journals and Correspondence* which he edited in 1841, and reprinted in 1932
by Mr R. G. Howarth. A new transcript, the result of the joint labours of
Mr Edwin Chapell and Mr W. Matthews, was published in 1935 (*The
Tangier Papers of Samuel Pepys*, Navy Records Society Publications, vol.
LXXIII). That Pepys was still using shorthand for business purposes at this time
is clear from an entry on 13 September 1683, when he was "with my Lord
in his cabin, for him to write, in long-hand, from my short-hand notes, which I
read, my arguments for destroying Tangier, with which he is greatly pleased".

A letter found among the Pepys papers in the collection of Mr J. Eliot
Hodgkin suggests that Pepys's knowledge of shorthand matters may have been
laid under contribution in connection with the Popish Plot trials. It is dated
from the "Court at Winchester, August 30th, 1684", and was written by the
Earl of Sunderland to Roger L'Estrange, directing him in His Majesty's name
to discover the shorthand writer who took notes of the proceedings at the trials
of Ireland, the five Jesuits, and Langhorne, and also the transcribers who copied
the shorthand notes in full for the press, and to require them to produce the
original notes and copies and give account of them. This order was given because
questions had arisen as to the accuracy of several passages of the printed reports
of those trials.[1]

The collector's instinct was so highly developed in Pepys that it is not surprising to find him turning his attention to the literature of an art in which he
took a peculiar interest. With the possible exception of Elisha Coles, author of
The Newest, Plainest and the Shortest Short-Hand, 1674, who enumerated some
thirty authors of treatises on stenography most of which appear to have been in
his possession, Pepys is the first genuine collector of shorthand books of whom
we have any record. With one exception, the whole of Pepys's books on stenography are contained in five small volumes, uniformly bound. At the end of the
fifth volume he has carefully drawn up "A General Alphabet shewing, in
distinct Columns, yᵉ Authors of yᵉ severˡˡ Methods of Short-hand hitherto

[1] *Hist. MSS. Comm. 15th Report*, Appendix, pt. II, 1897, p. 178.

publish'd in England, & to be found in any of ye 5 Vols. thereof in this Collection." Here is the list just as it was written down by the diarist:

Addy Willm......		Rich, Jer's Pen's Dexterity in a Sheet	1659
Bale Pet^r's Brachygraphy	1590	D° vid { Botley	
Botley Saml upon Rich's Method	1674	{ Stringer	
Bridges Noah	1659	Ridpath Geo	1687
Bright Tim M. D.	1588	Shelton Tho. his, vizt	
Coles E.	1674	Tachygraphy, the last }	1691
Dix Hen	1641	of numerous Editions }	
Everardt Job	1658	La^{tn} Translation of D°	1671
Farthing John	1684	Tutor to it	1642
Folkingham W^m 2 edn	1622	Zeiglographia	1685
Heath Tho	1644	Slater Tho: upon Nicholas's Method	1692
Mason Willm his, vizt		Steel Lawr.	1678
Pen frõ an Eagle's Wing	1673	Stringer Nath upon Rich his Method	1686
Art's Advancement	1682	Willis { Edm^d 2^d edition	1627
Metcalfe Theoph.'s Radio- }	1690	{ John B. D. his, vizt	
steno^{phy}; last edition }		Stenography { 6th edition	1619
Nicholas Abr. *Vid.* Slater		{ 12th edit	1639
Ramsay C. A. in Fr^{ch} & Lat^n }	1680	School M^{ar} { 2nd edit	1628
dedic^{ted} to ye K^g of Fr^{ce} }		to D° { 3rd edit	1647

It would seem that Pepys made diligent enquiry for shorthand works, for he has written out a list of "Short-Hands wanting of ye Catalogue given us by E. Coles in his Treatise on that Subject 1674, as not being (after 2 Years Search) to be any where found at the Closing of this my Collection thereof March 25th 1695". The list is as under:

Bale's New-Year's Gift for England	Rich his Bookes
Bartlet	{ S.
Beecher	Shelton { T.'s Continuation of his Tachy-
Button	{ graphy
Facy	Stileman
Hopkins	Walker
Labourer	West
Metcalfe's Schoole-Ma^r to his Radio-Steno-	Willoughby
graphy	Witt
Ratcliffe	

An earlier list of "Shorthands yet Wanting", written by Pepys on the back of a sheet of notes and dated January 1693/4, was found by Mr O. F. Morshead loosely inserted in the Pepysian copy of Elias Ashmole's *Institution...of...the Garter*, 1672 (No. 2574). It appears from this list that Pepys's collection then lacked copies of Bright's *Characterie*, Bales's *Writing Schoolemaster*, the systems of the two Willises, Dix, Everardt and Mason, as well as Rich's broadsheet and Shelton's Latin *Tachygraphia*. These books must have been acquired, therefore, between January 1694 and March 1695.

Of the books which eluded Pepys's search a number are to be found in various public and private libraries, some are known only from their appearance on the Registers of the Stationers' Company, whilst others have vanished without leaving any trace other than the names of their authors as given by Coles. In this connection it may be noted that Coles wrote: "Some of these I have not been able to meet with. Som came too late to hand, & som are onely ready for the press."

A copy of Peter Bales's *New-yeares Gift for England*, 1600, apparently unique, was located by the compiler of the present catalogue in the Bibliothèque Nationale, Paris (see p. 9)

Nothing is known of a shorthand treatise by Bartlet apart from Coles's list.

John Westby Gibson (*Bibliography of Shorthand*, 1887, p. 20) suggests that Coles's "Beecher" is probably J. J. Becher, author of "Character pro notitia linguarum universali inventum steganographicum hactenus inauditum", Frankfurti, 1661; but the reference may be to the Edward Beecher who contributed, as did Coles himself, some laudatory verses to William Hopkins's *The Flying Pen-Man, or the Art of Short-Writing*, 1674 (see below).

"Button" is perhaps a misprint for "Burton". An engraved handbill dated 1688, of which a copy is preserved in the Bagford collection in the British Museum, shows that Moses Burton was a teacher of Addy's stenography at the Hand and Pen in Red Cross Street. The handbill is reproduced in Alexander T. Wright's *Jeremiah Rich*, 1911.

The only known copy of William Facy's *Complement of Stenography*, 1672, is preserved in the Washington Library of Congress (Z 56, F 14). The full title is given in Julius Ensign Rockwell's *Teaching, Practice and Literature of Shorthand*, Washington, 1884.

Two editions of William Hopkins's *The Flying Pen-Man, or the Art of Short-Writing* are extant, copies of both being in the British Museum. The first edition (7942.a.12) bears the imprint: "London, Printed by C. H. for the Author: At the Golden Ball in St. Mathew's Court, near the Nag's head Tavern In Cheapside A° 1674." It was announced in the "Term Catalogue" for Hilary 1674/5 (*T.C.* I, 198). Another edition, without date, was printed for "Samvel Lee at yᵉ Feathers in Lumbart Street near yᵉ Post Office" and announced in the "Term Catalogue" for Hilary 1680 (*T.C.* I, 386). A copy of this edition is in the Bodleian (302.g.151).

A work by William Laborer entitled *The Arte of Short English Writing* was entered on the Stationers' Register to George Elde and Miles Flesher on 15 March 1620/21 (*Arber's Transcript*, IV, 50), but although Thomas Gurney would appear to have seen a copy of this book about the middle of the eighteenth century (it is mentioned in the "Postscript" to the fourth edition of his *Brachygraphy, c.* 1760) none is known to be extant now.

Theophilus Metcalfe's *Schoolmaster to Radio-Stenography* was first published in 1649 by John Hancock, "at the first shop in Popes-Head-alley, next to Cornhill". The only perfect copy recorded is in the British Museum (7942.a.20). An incomplete one is in the Earl of Crawford's Library at Haigh Hall, Wigan. A second edition appeared in 1668, of which there are copies in the Chetham Library, Manchester, and the National Library of Scotland (see p. 53).

Thomas Ratcliff was the author of *The Art of Short-writing by Characters, fair, short, swift, easie, and legible. First invented by J. Willis, afterwards more illustrated by H. Dix, and now more largely composed and compleated; With an additional table of words, and every way made easie to the meanest capacity. By Tho. Ratcliff. London, Printed by Thomas Johnson at the Golden Key in St. Pauls-Churchyard.* No copy of this book is known to be in existence, but it was advertised at the end of A'ΥΘΕ'ΝΤΗΣ, *or a treatise of self-deniall*, by Theophilus Polwheile, M.A., 1658. Another work by Ratcliff, entitled *A New Art of Short and Swift Writing without Characters*, was published posthumously in 1688 with a preface by Thomas Cross, who engraved a frontispiece for the first edition. A perfect copy is in the Carlton collection and a mutilated one in the National Library of Scotland (Warden collection, Wn.1622²). The second edition, announced in the "Term Catalogue" for Easter 1693 (*T.C.* II, 459), contained a new frontispiece by F. H. Van Hove, to whom the authorship of the book was erroneously ascribed by J. Westby Gibson (*Bibliography of Shorthand*, 1887, p. 223). There are two copies of this edition in the British Museum. The third edition, dated 1711, is also in the British Museum and in the Carlton collection. For further information concerning Ratcliff and his works, see A. Tremaine Wright's "*Mr. Ratcliff of Plimouth*" *and Thomas Cross*, 1907, and *Addenda*, 1909.

"Rich his Bookes" on shorthand were at least three in number, and it is surprising that the Pepysian collection contains none of them, nor of the four or five editions of Rich's system published after the author's death but prior to 1695, although Pepys had a copy of Rich's broadside *The Pens Dexterity*. Particulars of the books will be found on pp. 58–9.

Samuel Shelton (the "S. Shelton" of Coles's list) was a pupil but apparently no kinsman of Thomas Shelton, the tachygrapher. His manual entitled *Brachygraphy, or the Art of Short-Writing* was "printed for Peter Parker, at the first shop in Popes-head-alley, on the right hand going out of Cornhill, 1672". Two copies are extant: one in the British Museum (7944.aa.34) and one in the Washington Library of Congress (Z56.S544), the latter having a portrait of the author prefixed.

"T. Shelton's Continuation of his Tachygraphy" is doubtless a reference to the following work entered on the Stationers' Register on 19 February 1683/4 (Roxb. *Transcript*, III, 225) and announced in the "Term Catalogue" for Michaelmas 1684: "The Art of Short-writing according to Tachy-graphy, first composed by Mr. Thomas Shelton, and approved by both Universities.... Also Mr. Jeremy Rich his method of contractions." A copy of the first edition is in the Carlton collection, imperfect copies are in the British Museum (1042.c.32) and Manchester Free Reference Library (Bailey collection, 514.K.73). The Bagford collection of title-pages in the British Museum includes the title-page of another edition dated 1696.

"Stileman" is unknown to shorthand bibliographers apart from Coles's list, but a unique copy of his book is in the Carlton collection. Its title is "Shorthand Shortned, Or, The Art of Short-Writing Very much Abreviated and facilitated, by the Industry and long experience of Robert Stileman Writing-Master. At the hand and Pen....London. Printed for the Author, 1673."

No shorthand work by a seventeenth-century Walker is known. Coles places this author between Folkingham (1620) and Bridges (1659).

Simon West, a London bookseller, was the author of *Arts Improvement: or, Short and Swift Writing*, London, 1647. The book was entered to West on the Stationers' Register on 1 December 1646 (Roxb. *Transcript*, I, 255) and its full title is given in Westby Gibson's *Bibliography of Shorthand*. There are copies in the British Museum (12991.cc.49) and the National Library of Scotland (Warden collection, Wn.876, incomplete).

An entry on the Stationers' Register to George Eld and Miles Flesher on 8 June 1621 relates to "A book of Stenography written by Edward Willoughby" (Arber's *Transcript*, IV, 55). As Mr A. T. Wright has pointed out (*William Folkingham*, 1898, p. 57), it is not improbable that no work was actually published, as the entry was "crost out with the consent of fflesher and order of a Court, holden the 6. of March 1621 [*i.e.* 1622]". "Willoughby's Art of Short-writing, 1621", is mentioned in William Massey's *The Origin and Progress of Letters*, 1763, but nothing more is known of such a work.

"Witt" is unknown to bibliographers save for the mention of his work by Coles. On 27 February 1632/3 "a booke called Brachygraphia or Short Writing, by Thomas Whiting", was entered on the Stationers' Register to Miles Flesher (Arber's *Transcript*, IV, 292), and Mr A. T. Wright has suggested (*Thomas Shelton, Tachygrapher*, 1896, p. 7) that the Whiting of the Register is perhaps the Witt of Coles. However that may be, no copy of a shorthand book by Whiting or Witt has yet been traced.

Pepys had a penchant for replacing early editions of his books by later ones when he could procure them. But for this foible it is possible that the first editions of Shelton and Metcalfe, of which no copies are now known to exist, might have been found on his shelves. In one case, however, that of Thomas Heath's manual, Pepys fortunately preserved the first edition of 1644 of which no other exemplar is known, a unique copy of the edition of 1664 being in the Bodleian Library. The diarist had two copies of the same edition of Metcalfe's *Short Writing*, called the nineteenth on the engraved title and the "last" on the letterpress title. At the foot of one of these he has written: "N.B.—that a useless Double hereof is by mistake to be found Pag. 297."

Some four years after the transfer of the Pepysian Library to Cambridge it was visited by Ralph Leycester, squire of Toft near Knutsford, Cheshire. Leycester was an enthusiastic disciple of John Byrom, the inventor of a system of shorthand which marked an important stage in the evolution of the art and the writer of a shorthand diary which, if it lacks the engaging candour of Pepys's chronicle, has a distinct charm of its own. Byrom's journal shows him to have been keenly interested in everything relating to stenography and, like Pepys, a collector of shorthand literature. Knowing this, his friend Leycester wrote to him on 22 May 1728:

"I spent the last week at Cambridge. Whilst I was there, I went to see a curious collection of books bequeathed to Magdalene College by the late Mr. Pepys. In the catalogue I met with a book entitled *Shorthand Collection*, and would gladly have seen it, but the gentleman who showed us the library being a stranger, and unacquainted with the method of the catalogue, we could not find it. Mr. Haderton[1] tells me it is a collection of shorthand books containing above a hundred and fifty different methods.[2] In searching for this book we found five large volumes quarto, being a journal of Mr. Pepys; I did not know the method, but they were writ very plain, and the proper names in common characters. If you think it worth your while to make Cambridge in your way to London, you will meet with these and I doubt not several other shorthand curiosities in the Magdalene Library. I had not time, and was loth to be troublesome to the library keeper, otherwise I would have deciphered some of the journal."[3]

A month later Leycester again wrote to Byrom: "Mr. Haderton promised me to send you a list of shorthand authors in Pepys' library as soon as possible; if I can get any sight of them I will do it when I am there."[4]

In May 1729 Byrom himself spent a few days in Cambridge, and he stayed there from the following November to 25 March 1730; but if he availed himself of the opportunity to examine the treasures of the Pepysian Library his journal is silent on the subject. This is the more inexplicable as the diary records several meetings at which Byrom discussed shorthand affairs with his pupils, a visit to the University in the company of the Librarian, Mr Haderton, and a visit to Clare Hall where he saw "Gruter's shorthand" (*i.e.* the ponderous tome of Jean Gruter on the Tironian notes).

---

[1] Samuel Hadderton was University Librarian from 1721 to 1731.

[2] A singular over-estimate. It is clear from Pepys's "General Alphabet" that he did not possess more than one-fifth of the number of shorthand books here stated.

[3] *The Private Journal and Literary Remains of John Byrom*, vol. I, pt. I, 1854, pp. 301-2 (Chetham Society, vol. xxxii). An indication of the close friendship between Leycester and Byrom is found in the following extract from a letter dated 14 October 1727, playfully announcing the squire's intention to take to himself a wife: "As I would act nothing contrary to the principles of shorthand and the allegiance I owe the Grand Master [*i.e.* Byrom], I would not for the world be so rash as to undertake an affair of this nature without first consulting your Highness, and therefore send you this epistle to beg that you will testify unto me your royal assent and approbation by some gracious signal: for if I can but obtain your consent, and the consent of one Catherine Norris a spinster, I'm determined for once in my life to play the fool and marry." (*Op. cit.*, p. 269.)

[4] *Ibid.* pp. 313-14.

Nearly a century afterwards John Nichols, F.S.A., referred to Pepys's shorthand books in his *Literary Anecdotes of the Eighteenth Century*[1] in the following terms: "Mr. Pepys' library contains everything that is wanting in the other libraries, so as to be their complement. To instance in a small particular: in three or more volumes, according to their sizes, he has collected almost every writer on short-hand, with a complete catalogue of all that he could ever hear of." Hartshorne's *Book Rarities of the University of Cambridge*, 1829, p. 262, merely mentions "four volumes of tracts on short hand" in an account of the Pepysian Library, but gives no details of them.

Despite the attention thus drawn to it at different times, Pepys's small but important collection of stenographiana, which includes some of the rarest books on the subject, had escaped the notice of shorthand bibliographers until recent years. The present volume represents an attempt to fill a gap in the catalogues of the special collections in which the Pepysian Library is so rich, as well as a contribution towards a reliable and comprehensive bibliography of English shorthand. For generous help afforded to its compiler at various stages of its progress my sincere thanks are tendered to the Pepysian Librarian, Mr F. McD. C. Turner, and his two predecessors in that office, Mr Owen F. Morshead, Librarian of Windsor Castle, and Sir Stephen Gaselee, Librarian of the Foreign Office. I am also indebted to the late Dr R. B McKerrow and the late Mr F. Sidgwick for many valuable suggestions.

[1] Vol. IV, p. 551 *n.* (1812).

W. J. CARLTON

GENEVA
April 1940

CATALOGUE OF THE SHORTHAND BOOKS IN THE LIBRARY OF SAMUEL PEPYS

Characterie. | An Arte | of shorte, swifte, | *and secrete wri-* |ting by Charac- | ter. | *Jnuented by Timothe* | Bright, Doctor of | Phisike. | [Ornament] | *Jmprinted at London by* | I. Windet, the Assigne | of Tim. Bright. | 1588. | Cum priuilegio Regiæ Maiestatis. | *Forbidding all other to print* | *the same.* [13.]

$4\frac{3}{4} \times 2\frac{1}{2}$ in., 24mo, pp. (256) letterpress, Roman and italic letter. With headlines, no numbers to pages. Sign. A12, B6,¶6, A–G12, H6, I12, K2. Shorthand characters inserted in MS. *S.T.C.* 3743.

Leaf 1ª Title, 1ᵇ blank, 2ª–6ª Dedication to Queen Elizabeth, 6ᵇ blank, 7ª–8ᵇ Instruction to the reader, 9ª–18ᵇ The arte of characterie, 19ª–24ª The characterie table, 24ᵇ blank, 25ª–114ᵇ A table of English wordes, 115ª–128ᵇ Appelative words. A folding sheet entitled "A generall vievv of the Art of Charactery" is found in some copies between leaves 8 and 9. The Pepysian copy does not contain this folding sheet.

Other copies are located as under:

(1) C.L.W. This copy is in the original vellum binding and contains the "generall vievv". It bears the autographs of James Bindley, 1812, and of Benjamin Hanbury. At the sale of Bindley's library on 10 December 1818 it was purchased by Hanbury for £3. 11s. and was still in his possession in November 1856 (cf. *Notes and Queries*, 2nd ser., XLVI, 393).

(2) B.L.O. (Douce W. 3). It bears the autographs of Peter Osborne, James Wilkinson and William Herbert, and the bookplate of Francis Douce. It lacks the "generall vievv". This copy is described by Herbert in his edition of Ames's "Typographical Antiquities", II, 1226–7 and note. It was bequeathed to the Bodleian with Douce's library in 1834. An article by Madeleine Doran on *Manuscript Notes in the Bodleian copy of Bright's* "*Characterie*" (*The Library*, XIV, 418–424, 1936) suggests that some of the notes may be in Bright's own hand.

(3) Salisbury Cathedral Library (O.2.53). This copy lacks the "generall vievv". It is bound in boards covered with old leather.

(4) A copy in the original vellum binding and containing the "generall vievv", formerly the property of Sir Francis Willughby, was purchased by Messrs Quaritch, Ltd., for £70 at the sale of Lord Middleton's library from Wollaton Hall, Nottingham, on 15 June 1925.

(5) A copy, lacking the "generall vievv", belonged to the Shakespearean scholar Thomas Caldecott, and at the sale of his library was purchased by Thorp on 9 December 1833 for £1. 18s. It afterwards formed part of the library of S. R. Christie-Miller, Britwell Court, Burnham, Bucks. At the sale of the Britwell Court library at Sotheby's on 15 March 1926 it was purchased by Abraham Rosenbach, Philadelphia, for £510.

A typographical reprint of "Characterie", with engraved shorthand characters and an additional leaf of "Advertisement" dated 26 July 1888, was edited by James Herbert Ford, *Reporters' Journal* Office, 27 Chancery Lane, London, W.C. 100 copies only were done. Although the editor claims to have followed the original "in every detail", this reprint is unreliable. In addition to a number of errors in the text, the omission of a word from the "characterie table" and the misreading of others, many shorthand characters are placed opposite words they do not represent.

Bright's was the first printed manual of shorthand in any language. Although its author was acquainted with the Roman *notæ*, whose invention he ascribes to Cicero, and his characters bear some resemblance to those of the monk John of Tilbury, *c*. 1180 (Arundel MS. 165), the system is an original one. Its basis consisted of 536 "charactericall" or key words, for which as many shorthand symbols were provided. These were formed from straight strokes differentiated by initial dashes, hooks and loops corresponding to the letters of the alphabet, *q* and *x* being omitted and the groups *ck, ijy, sz, uvw* each represented by a single sign. To each of these characters different appendages could be attached, and they could be written in four directions. Any character could stand not only for a "primitive" word, such as a noun, but also for "derivatives" such as verbs and adjectives, and all inflections both

2

of the primitive and derivatives. Tenses were distinguished in some cases by dots. The plural of nouns was shown by a dot at the side of the character, and the negative by a stroke through it. Any character might also represent, by what Bright called the "consenting" or "dissenting" method, either a synonym or a word of opposite meaning. For a synonym, the shorthand symbol representing the initial of the word required was written on the left of the key word; for a word of opposite meaning the shorthand initial was written on the right. The student was instructed, however, that "the sence onlie is to be taken with the character, whē besides that wee desire to bee swift, the very expresse worde is not necessarie". In accordance with this rule, words might be omitted and a paraphrase substituted for the *ipsissima verba*. In addition to his 536 "charactericall" words, Bright provided a number of "particles" for certain pronouns, prepositions and other words of frequent occurrence, on the lines of the "grammalogues" of modern systems. A peculiar feature of the system is that it was written from top to bottom of the page instead of from left to right.

Bright's shorthand is fully described and analysed by Paul Friedrich in "Studien zur englischen Stenographie im Zeitalter Shakespeares" (Sonderabdruck aus *Archiv für Schriftkunde*, Jahrg. 1, Nr. 2/3, 1914). The best description in English is Edward Pocknell's "Timothy Bright's, or the first English, Shorthand, 1588" (reprinted from *Shorthand*, 11, 126–32, 1884).

TIMOTHY BRIGHT (1550?–1615), son of William Bright, was born at Cambridge, where he matriculated as a subsizar of Trinity College on 21 May 1561, "imp[ubes] 11". He was admitted a Scholar of Trinity in 1567 and graduated B.A. in 1568. He went out of residence about 1570 without taking his M.A. degree and studied medicine on the continent. In 1572 he was in Paris, escaping the massacre of St Bartholomew only by taking refuge in the house of the British ambassador, Sir Francis Walsingham, and it was probably about this time that he visited the mineral springs at Spa.

In 1574 he took his M.B. degree at Cambridge, and in 1579 became M.D. He settled in Cambridge after his marriage and practised in his profession. There he wrote his first book, "A Treatise wherein is declared the sufficiencie of English medicines, for cure of all diseases, cured with medicine." The title sufficiently indicates its purport. It was printed at London in 1580, with a dedication to Lord Zouch signed "T. B." but no other indication of its author. Bright was then living in the parish of St Mary-the-Great, where three of his children were baptised. In 1583 another medical work in Latin, with Bright's name on the title-page, appeared in two parts entitled respectively "Hygieina" and "Therapeutica". Both parts were dedicated to Lord Burghley, with whom he seems to have been well acquainted. By 1584 Bright had removed to Ipswich, where his son Peter was baptised at St Mary-at-the-Quay. Here he penned the dedication to Sir Philip Sidney of his next book, "In physicam Gulielmi Adolphi Scribonii", printed at the Cambridge University Press in 1584. He had met Sidney for the first time twelve years before in the house of Sir F. Walsingham at Paris, "id[que] illa Gallicis Ecclesiis funesta tēpestate (cuius pars fui, et animus meminisse horret, luctuque refugit) matutinis Parisiensibus".

Backed by recommendations from Burghley, Walsingham and Sir Walter Mildmay, Bright was appointed physician of St Bartholomew's Hospital in 1585 at a stipend of 40s. a year, with a house and garden in "little St Bartlemewes by Smithfield". His "Treatise of Melancholy", a book to which Burton acknowledges indebtedness and which Shakespeare is said to have laid under contribution for his study of Hamlet, was printed in 1586. A second edition appeared in the same year, and a third in 1613. The book is as much metaphysical as medical, and the later chapters are concerned almost exclusively with religious melancholy.

In March 1586, Vincent Skinner, who had been Bright's tutor at Cambridge, wrote to Sir Michael Hicks, one of Burghley's secretaries, announcing that his quondam pupil had "enterprised a matter of rare noveltie and effected it", and enclosing a specimen of Bright's newly invented shorthand—"a matter of great vse and commoditie, to couch much matter in so short compasse and to take a speech from any man's mouth as he delivereth it". Skinner observed that the doctor was "desirous to haue some effectuall frute of his travayle, having charg of [a] familie and his profession yelding him small mayntenaunce as yet", and recommended that "som priviledg be geven him by hir ma^{tie} for the onely teaching of this his own invention, and the printing of such things as shall be taken by that means". In July 1588 Elizabeth granted to her well-beloved subject Timothy Bright and to his assigns letters patent "to

4

teach imprinte and publishe. . .in or by Character not before this tyme comonly
knowen & vsed by any other our subiects" for the space of fifteen years, and
soon afterwards his shorthand system was made public in a book entitled "Characterie", dedicated to the Queen. Various sermons by Stephen Egerton, Anthony
Tyrrell and Henry Smith, printed between 1589 and 1591, purported to have
been "taken by characterie", and it has been conjectured that Bright's shorthand
was instrumental in the production of the "bad" quartos of Shakespeare's
plays.

In 1589 Bright produced an abridgment of Foxe's "Book of Martyrs", and
in dedicating it to Sir F. Walsingham he again recalled the tragic event which
had left so lasting an impression. "Among all your honourable fauours", he
wrote, "that especiall protection from the bloudy massacre of Paris, nowe
sixteene yeeres passed: yet (as euer it will bee) fresh with mee in memory: hath
alwaies since bound me, with all the bondes of duetie, and seruice vnto your
honour. . . . As then you were the very hand of God to preserue my life, so
haue you (ioyning constancie with kindnes) been a principall means, wherby
the same hath beene the better sustained."

Bright's theological leanings were emphasised by his appointment, early in
1590, as one of the curates of Christ Church, Newgate Street, and on 19 July
he was preferred to the rectory of Stanford Rivers, Essex, but does not appear
to have been instituted. The claims of theology and stenography may have
absorbed too much of his time, and he was repeatedly admonished for neglecting
his duties to the poor patients of the hospital. The warnings seem to have gone
unheeded, his supply of "billetts & coles" was stopped, and at Michaelmas 1591
he was dismissed from his post. A month previously he had been instituted to
the rectory of Methley, near Wakefield, and thither he must have travelled
with his family immediately after being released from his duties at St Bartholomew's. As early as July 1591 he had signed an agreement undertaking, in the
event of his vacating the parsonage, to support the nominee of John (afterwards
Sir John) Savile, Lord of the Manor of Methley, and had pledged himself to
secrecy concerning this dubious pact. At Methley Bright's father died in 1592.
The new rector soon became involved in disputes with his parishioners about
the payment of tithe, the Lord of the Manor taking sides against the parson,
whom he accused of leaving his charge destitute in order to practise medicine.
Petitions and counter-petitions followed one another in quick succession, until

in 1597 Bright was summoned before an ecclesiastical commission at York and ordered to contribute the fortieth part of his benefice towards the relief of the poor. He had gone through the form of resignation of the living in 1594, but for some reason the resignation was inoperative. In the same year he was presented to the rectory of Barwick-in-Elmet, the most valuable of all the livings in the gift of the Duchy of Lancaster, and thus became a pluralist. To Barwick he appears to have moved in due course, and his son Peter was buried there in 1595. It was apparently Bright's custom to spend a part of the summer season at Harrogate. He was one of the first to recognise the medicinal value of the mineral springs there, gave it the name of the English Spa, and projected a work in praise of the Harrogate waters which he did not live to write.

At some date which cannot be definitely fixed the author of "Characterie" migrated to Shrewsbury, where his brother William Bright, of Emmanuel College, Cambridge, had been since 1598 public preacher and incumbent of St Mary's Church. There he spent his closing years and made his will on 9 August 1615. It reveals him to have been a lover of music and an accomplished instrumentalist, as well as a linguist of no mean calibre. His favourite instruments were the theorbo and the Irish harp. He held the livings of Methley and Barwick until his death, and was buried at St Mary's, Shrewsbury, on 6 September 1615, his brother being interred there three years later and his widow Margaret in 1620.

Some fragments of the stenographic seal which Bright used for his correspondence have been preserved. It depicts a winged hand holding a quill which has traced three charactery symbols, surrounded by the legend "Timotheus. Bright. Ingenio. Arte. Manu."

Bright's eldest son, Timothy, who was apparently estranged from his father, adopted the law as his profession. The name Timothy was bestowed in turn upon his eldest son and one of his grandchildren, whilst another grandchild became the mother of William Congreve, the dramatist.

(W. J. Carlton's *Timothe Bright, Doctor of Phisicke: a Memoir of "The Father of Modern Shorthand"*, 1911; *D.N.B.*; *Yorkshire Archæological Journal*, XVII, 50–4, 1903; Ven. H. A. Hall's "Dr Timothy Bright: Some Troubles of an Elizabethan Rector" (reprinted from the Thoresby Society's *Miscellanea*, XV, 30–7, 1905).)

The | VVriting Schoolemaster: | Conteining three Bookes in one; The first, tea- | *ching* Swift writing; *The second,* True wri- | ting; *The third,* Faire writing. | [Ornament] | *The first Booke, Entituled;* | The Arte Of Brachygraphie: that is, to | write as fast as a man speaketh treatably, writing but one | *letter for a word: Verie commodious for the generall encrease* | *and furtherance of learning in all Estates and degrees: the* | *knowledge whereof may easilie be attained by one mo-* | neths studie, and the performance by one moneths | practise. The proofe alreadie made by | diuers Schollers there- | in. | *The second Boooke: Named,* | The Order Of Orthographie: shewing | the perfect Method to write true Orthographie in our | *English tongue, as it is now generally printed, vsed,* | and allowed, of the best & most learned Writers: | To be attained by the right vse of this Booke | without a Schoolemaster, in short | time, and with small paines, | by your owne priuate | studies. | *The Third Booke; is,* | The Key Of Calygraphie: opening the rea- | die waie to write faire in verie short time, by the ob- | *seruations of necessarie Rules here set downe, and* | by the imitation of the best examples that may | be procured. | Inuented by *Peter Bales.* 1. Ianu. 1590. | *Omne bonum, Dei donum.* | Imprinted at London by *Thomas Orwin:* and are to be | solde at the Authors house in the vpper ende of the | *Old Bayly, where he teacheth the said Artes.* [1111¹.]

7½ × 5¼ in., 4to, pp. (132) letterpress, partly in **B.L.** With headlines, no numbers to pages. Sign. A–A2, B–I4, K–R4 in fours. Dots and dashes inserted in MS. *S.T.C.* 1312.

Leaf 1ª–1ᵇ blank, 2ª Title, 2ᵇ Arms and crest of Sir Christopher Hatton (A1), 3ª Dedication to Sir C. Hatton, 3ᵇ To the Reader (A2), 4ª–4ᵇ Latin and English verses by Thomas Newton, P. Hunsdon and Thomas Lodge (B1), 5ª–6ᵇ Preface (B2–3), 7ª Authoris: In Artem Brachygraphiae suam, 7ᵇ blank (B4), 8ª The authors censure of his first booke, 8ᵇ blank (C1), 9ª–11ᵇ The first booke, Intituled: The Arte of Brachygraphie: that is, of short writing (C2–C4), 12ª–14ᵇ The Table of Brachygraphie (D1–D3), 15ª–15ᵇ Words most vsuall and common (D4), 16ª–16ᵇ The order of Orthographie (E1), 17ª–17ᵇ The Table of the Christen or proper names

(E2), 18ᵃ–60ᵇ The Table for Orthographie, and for the references of words, to the Table of Brachygraphie (E3–Q1), 61ᵃ–65ᵇ The Key of Calygraphie (Q2–R2), 66ᵃ The Booke to the Reader and The Author to his Countrimen in verse, 66ᵇ–67ᵇ blank (R3–4).

Bales's "Writing Schoolmaster" was entered on the Register of the Stationers' Company to Thomas Orwyn on 1 December 1589 (Arber's *Transcript*, II, 535). The Pepysian copy, which is bound with other works in the fifth volume of the shorthand collection, is imperfect, lacking leaves D2, I3, I4, R3, R4. It has been cut down to 7 × 4½ in.

Other copies are located as under:

(1) B.L.O. (Douce B. subt. 228). It bears the autograph of Wm. Herbert, April 1773, and the bookplate of Francis Douce, by whom it was bequeathed to the Bodleian in 1834.

(2) U.L.C. (Dd*.3.43¹ (E)). This copy bears on the title-page the autograph of John Hackett (1592–1670), Bishop of Coventry and Lichfield, and on the verso of R4 that of John Webster (qy. the dramatist, who refers to brachygraphy in "The Deuils Law-case", 1623, Act IV, Scene ii).

(3) L.P.L. (xxxi.1.36: in the original vellum binding).

(4) C.L.M. (with autograph of J. Byrom, 3.F.1.3. wanting the last two leaves).

(5) F.L.W. (Harmsworth coll.).

An edition was printed in 1597 with the following title: "The Arte | Of Brachygraphie: | *that is,* | To write as fast as a man | speaketh treatably, writing but | one letter for a word. | With sundry new additions, since the | first edition, and better helpes for the | ease of the said Arte: | The Order of Orthographie, most | brieflie set down, for the speedie | writing of true English: | The Key of Kalygraphie, opening the | readie way to write faire: In briefe | rules deliuered. | 10. Octobris. 1597. | *Arte, & vsu,* *Penna.* P. Bales. | ♣ Imprinted at London by | George Shawe and Ralph Blower, | for Thomas Charde. | An. Dom. 1597." Sign. A–E12 in twelves. Dedicated to Lord Hunsdon. The only recorded copy is in B.L.O. (8° B. 76. Art). *S.T.C.* 1311.

The section relating to brachygraphy was reissued under the title: "*A New-yeares gift* | for England. | *The Art of new Brachygraphie*. | Verie necessarie to be learned and | written with great speede: by the | abbreuiation of all English words | into three or foure letters with a | tittle, for the lōgest words. | *Verie conuenient, profitable, and necessary for* | *young students in* Diuinitie, Law, Phisicke, | *and* Philosophie: *in the speedie furthe-* | *rance and ease of their studies.* | Wherby a man may take a Sermon, or any | other speech *verbatim* as fast as a man spea- | keth treatably: as hath bin tryed by | diuerse practisers therein. | *Quod facis fac cito. Mora trahit periculum.* | *Deuised by* Peter Bales *of London Gent.* | 1. Ianuarij. Anno. 1600. | *London,* | Printed by Richard Field. | 1600." Sign. A–Exii in twelves. This work was entered on the Stationers' Register to Edmond Bolifant and Arnalt Hatfield on 10 Nov. 1599 (Arber's *Transcript*, III, 150). The only recorded copy is in B.N.P. (p. V. 474).

Bales's brachygraphy was not a system of shorthand in the modern sense of the term. His method was to represent words by writing a "prick" or "tittle" in different positions in relation to the letters of the ordinary alphabet. These "pricks" or "tittles" were of four kinds: a dot, a comma, a short and a long dash, and to each of them twelve positions were assigned, so that each letter could be made to stand for 48 words. Bales's "table of brachygraphie" is merely a reprint of the 536 words listed in Timothy Bright's "Characterie", 1588 (see p. 2).

PETER BALES (1547–1610?), eldest son of Thomas and Elizabeth Bales of Birchin Lane, Cornhill, was baptised at St Michael's, Cornhill, 15 June 1547. His father was a London draper. According to Joseph Campion (*The Parallel; or, Comparative Penmanship Exemplified*, 1749), he was already practising penmanship "about 1559". He is said by Anthony Wood to have been connected with Gloucester (now St Edmund) Hall, Oxford, where his calligraphic skill attracted attention. Holinshed records that on 10 August 1575 he presented Queen Elizabeth with a gold and crystal ring containing in microscopic writing the Lord's Prayer, the Creed, the Ten Commandments, two Latin prayers, his "posie", his name, the day of the month, the year of our Lord and of the Queen's reign, in a circle the size of a penny. The Queen is

9

said to have greatly admired this piece of work and to have worn the ring on several occasions. A petition of Bales's son John, citizen and draper of London, shows that Peter Bales had been tutor to Prince Henry (*Hist. MSS. Comm. Appendix to 4th Report*, 1874, p. 42). In a suit in which he was called as a witness in 1582 he is described as "servant to the Archbishop of Canterbury" (Town Depositions, 179, P.R.O.). Bales's services were utilised by his patrons, Sir F. Walsingham and Sir C. Hatton, in affairs of State which entailed the deciphering and copying of secret correspondence. Some work fell to him in connection with the discovery of Babington's plot in 1586.

In 1590 Bales was living at the upper end of the Old Bailey next to the sign of the Dolphin, where he kept a writing school. He was employed about this time in transcribing public documents into book form (Harl. MS. 2368). The publication of his "Writing Schoolemaster" in 1590 led to a lawsuit in which Bales and his printer, Thomas Orwin, were concerned. He is described as "Peter Bales, of the parish of St Sepulchre, London, gent aged 44 or thereabouts". From the depositions it appears that 750 copies were printed, that their value was about £200, and that Bales "had sold many of the said books for 10 groats a book". Despite the intervention of his friend Peter Ferriman, who wrote on his behalf to Sir Thomas Randolph, his hopes of appointment to a permanent post were not realised. He petitioned Lord Burghley for the post of York Herald, apparently unsuccessfully, and in 1592 enlisted the support of Sir John Puckering, Lord Keeper of the Great Seal. He contributed one of the plates in "Theatrum Artis Scribendi", engraved and published by Jodocus Hondius about 1594.

The publisher of George Ripley's "Compound of Alchymy", 1591, Ralph Rabbards, states that he was assisted in correcting Ripley's ill-written copy by "Peter Bales in the Olde Bayly, a most notable and experienced decipherer of olde and unperfect writing". Bales contributed eighteen lines of blank verse prefixed to the work.

On Michaelmas Day, 1595, Bales emerged victoriously from a contest with a younger rival, Daniel Johnson of "Paules Churchyarde, near the Bishops Palace", for a golden pen valued at £20, "wch Chalenge was divided into three partes: The first for best and fairest writing of all kinde of handes usuall: The second for Secretarie and Clerklike writing: The third for best teachinge". The scene of the trial was "at the Black Fryers, within the Conduit yard, next to the Pipe Office", and it was held in the presence of five judges and 100 spectators. After Bales's triumph the pen was "brought to his house by foure of the judges and delivered unto him absolutelie as his owne", and although Johnson printed an appeal, which he had posted all over the city, accusing Bales of having obtained possession of it "by subtill plottes, base practises, and sinister & cunning shifts", Bales justified himself in a book entitled "The Originall Cause", dated 1 January 1596, which appears never to have been published (Harl. MS. 675). The posting of bills was a form of publicity much in favour with writing masters and teachers of stenography about this time, and as no actual specimen is known to have been preserved the text of one of those issued by Bales, as given in the account of his contest with Johnson, is worth reproducing here:

"At the Signe of the Golden pen,
"In the vpper end of the old Bailie.

There dwelleth one that teacheth to write all manner of handes vsuall, after a more exact, vsefull, and speedie waye, then hath heretofore bene taught; as by Triall hathe bene latelie found by his Chalenge pformed therein, and in faire writing, for a penne of gold of twentie pound value, wch he wonne by the Censure of five severall Judges.

"There may you also learne to write as fast as a man speaketh treatablie, by the Arte of Brachigraphie, by him devised; writing but one letter for a Word; as hath bene tryed in manye of his Schollers.

"There may you have any thing faire written in any kinde of hand vsuall; and Bookes of Copies, such as you shall bespeake.

"There is also to be seene his Maister Piece, wherewith he wonne the Golden Pen: and other pieces of small writinge worth the sight.

"Arte, et vsu Penna. Soli Deo Gloria.
"God saue the Queene.   P. Bales."

Bales's exploit was celebrated in verse by Samuel Rowlands in "The Letting of Hvmours Blood in the Head-Vaine", 1600, and there is an allusion to Peter Bales's brachygraphy in Thomas Nash's "Summers Last Will and Testament" of the same date. (*Works*, ed. R. B. McKerrow, iii. 252, iv. 427.)

In 1598 a Mr Wyseman petitioned the Earl of Essex on Bales's behalf for "a clarke's place in the courte". He was employed in 1599 by John Danyell to copy some stolen letters written by the Earl of Essex to his Countess. The Earl was then in disgrace, and Danyell extorted a large sum from the Countess in return for the destruction of the letters, in which he had inserted passages of a treasonable character. A few weeks later Danyell refused Bales's request for a loan of £20, whereupon the latter drew up a full statement of the affair which he gave to the Countess. Danyell was tried in the Star Chamber on a charge of forgery, Bales giving evidence against him, and was sentenced to the pillory, a heavy fine and perpetual imprisonment.

In "The Scourge of Folly", 1610, John Davies included an epigram on his rival, whom he calls Clophonian, implying that Bales was then in needy circumstances and obliged to move from place to place to evade his creditors.

(*D.N.B.*; *Biographia Britannica*; W. Massey's *Origin and Progress of Letters*, 1763; Sir Edward Clarke's *Swifthand*, 1909; Alex. T. Wright's *Peter Bales' Brachygraphy* (1904) and *John Willis, S.T.B. and Edmond Willis*, 1926; Sir Ambrose Heal's *The English Writing-Masters*, 1931, pp. 9, 11, 128–9.)

The Art of | Stenographie: | *or*, | Short Writing. | Inuented by *Iohn Willis* batcheler in | *Diuinitie, and now fully perfected by* | the said Author for the true writing | *both of English, Latine, and all other* | *languages whatsoeuer.* | Seene and allowed according to order. | The sixt edition. | *Omne bonum dei donum.* | *Quisquis βομσολογων Mæandris deuius erras,* | *Huc ades: hic firma nititur arte liber.* | Imprinted at London for *Robert* | *Willis*, and are to be sould by *W.* | *Iones dwelling in Redcrosse-* | streete. 1618.   [402³.]

4¾ × 3⅛ in., 8vo, pp. (60) letterpress. With headlines. No numbers to pages. Sign. A2–8, B–D7 in eights. Shorthand characters in the text inserted in MS.

Leaf 1ᵃ Title, 1ᵇ Encomium scripturæ stenographica, a Marco Manilio lib. 4 [3 lines] and In Iohannis Willissi S.P. Sacræ Theologia Doctoris tetrasticon [4 lines], 2ᵃ–4ᵃ To the Reader . . . I.W., 4ᵇ blank, 5ᵃ–29ᵃ The Art of Stenographie, 29ᵇ The Art of Stenographie (contd.) and The Lord's Prayer and The Beliefe in shorthand characters, 30ᵃ The Ten Commandments in shorthand characters, 30ᵇ blank.

No other copy of this edition is recorded. Leaf A1 (probably a blank) is missing from the Pepysian copy.

The first edition was issued anonymously in 1602. It was entered on the Stationers' Register to Cuthbert Burby on 19 April 1602 (Arber's *Transcript*, III, 204). *S.T.C.* 25744ª. The *S.T.C.* entry under 25744 is a "ghost". The full title is as follows:

The Art of | Stenographie, | Teaching by plaine and certaine | Rules, to the capacitie of the | *meanest, and for the vse of* | all professions, *The* | *way of compendious* | *Writing.* | Wherevnto is annexed a very easie | direction for *Steganógraphie,* | or, Secret Writing. | Horat. serm. lib. 1. Satyr. 4. | *Si quid promittere de me* | *Possum aliud, verè promitto.* | [Woodcut device, McKerrow 165] | At London, | Printed for *Cuthbert Burbie.* | 1602.

Copies of this first edition are in B.M.L. (C.58.bb.20, wanting the folding sheet); B.L.O. (8° A. 26. Art. B5); C.C.O.; Staats- und Universitäts-bibliothek, Königsberg; and W.J.C. The Earl of Lonsdale's copy, sold at Sotheby's on 14 July 1937 for £70, is now in F.L.W.

No copies of the second, third and fourth editions are known to be extant.

A unique copy of the fifth edition, 1617, is in C.L.M. (Byrom coll., 3.E.7.66), consisting of 52 unnumbered letterpress pages. Sign. A–D2 in eights. With headlines. It bears the autograph signature of John Byrom. The full title of this edition is as follows:

The Art of | Stenographie: | or, | Short Writing. | Inuented by *Iohn Willis* batchelanr in | Diuinity: and now newly inlarged | by the said Author, with all | necessary additions, fit for the | better vnderstanding | thereof. | The fift Edition. | *Omne bonum Dei donum.* | *Quisquis βομσολόγων Mæandris deuius erras,* | *Huc ades: Hic Firmâ nititur arte liber.* | Imprinted at London by *W. White,* | dwelling in Cow-lane. | 1617.

On the last page of this edition is the colophon: "These Bookes are to be sold by *W. White* the printer thereof, dwelling in Cow-lane: And the Art taught by *Robert Willis,* who lodgeth at the house of *M. Dauies* without Ludgate." Robert Willis was entered on the Stationers' Register in respect of this book, "by assignement from master Welby", on 10 October 1617 (Arber's *Transcript,* III, 614).

No copy of the seventh edition has been located.

13

On 2 December 1622 Willis's "Art of Stenographie", which "formerlie was the Copie of Robert Willis, latelie Deceased", was assigned to Henry Seile (Arber's *Transcript*, IV, 87). In 1623 an eighth edition was issued by Seile with an engraved title-page, the work of Francis Delaram (Johnson, No. 7), in place of the letterpress title-page of the earlier editions. It shows a pretty pastoral scene, with shepherds and flock, etc., above which is the inscription: "Omne bonvm dei donvm", and below: "Viam breuissimam uel bruta sectantur." In an oval medallion which occupies the centre is the title, as follows:

The | Art of | Stenographie | *or Short Writing by* | *Spelling Characterie* | *Invented by Iohn Willis* | *Batcheler in Divinitie.* | *The Eighth Edition* | *Printed for Henry Seile &* | *are to be sold at his shop* | *the Tygers head in* | *Paules church* | *yard* | 1623.

The only recorded copies of the eighth edition are in J.R.G. (Todd coll.) and W.J.C.

The ninth edition has the same engraved title-page by Delaram prefixed, with the date altered to 1628. There is also a letterpress title-page which adds, after "*The Ninth Edition*": "Whereunto is now adioyned the *Schoolemaster* to the said *Art*, compleatly fitted for this ninth *Edition*, by the aforesaid *Authour*, a little before his death." Copies of this edition are in B.M.L. (1043.b.61, wanting the "Schoolmaster"); B.L.O. (8° W. 13. Art, wanting engraved title-page and engraved plates, with the "Schoolmaster", 2nd ed., 1628; and Mason AA.67, wanting engraved title-page and "Schoolmaster"); C.L.W. (Lewis and Walford colls., with the engraved title-page of the 10th ed., 1628, wanting the "Schoolmaster"); and B.N.P. (v, 55422, wanting the "Schoolmaster").

The tenth edition has similar engraved and letterpress title-pages, the date having been altered to 1632. Copies are in B.M.L. (Fraser coll., 1043.a.63, wanting engraved title-page and plate of "Defectives of the first, second, third and fourth sorts", with the "Schoolmaster", 2nd ed., 1628); L.C.W. (Blair coll., Z56.W735, with engraved title-page dated 1628); U.L.Y. (F25.135, with the "Schoolmaster", 2nd ed., 1628).

A copy of the eleventh edition, 1636, formerly in Dr Williams's Library, Gordon Square, London, W.C., is not now to be found there.

The Art of | Stenographie: | *or,* | *Short-Writing, by Spelling* | *Characterie.* | Invented by Jo. Willis, Bachelor | in Divinitie. | *The twelfth Edition.* | Whereunto is now adjoyned the *Schoole-* | *master* to the said *Art*, compleatly fitted | for this twelfth Edition, as it was done | by the afore-said Author, a little | before his death. | *Omne bonum Dei donum.* | London, | Printed for *Henry Seile*, at the Tygers head | in Fleetstreet, over against Saint | *Dunstans*-Church. 1639. [402¹⁰.]

5½ × 3⅜ in., 8vo, pp. (2) engraved, 32 letterpress and 5 engraved leaves printed on both sides. With headlines. No numbers to pages. Sign. A–B8 in eights. The shorthand characters inserted in the text are engraved. Colophon on last page: "London, | Printed for *Henry Seile*, at the Tygers head | in Fleetstreet, over against Saint | *Dunstans*-Church. 1639." The engraved title-page of the 10th edition, 1628, is prefixed. The "Schoolmaster" is not "adjoyned" to the Pepysian copy.

Leaf 1ª Engraved title, 1ᵇ Quisquis...Encomium...Tetrastichon, 2ª Letterpress title, 2ᵇ–3ª "To the Reader...I.W.", 3ᵇ–4ᵇ The Art of Stenographie, 5ª The alphabet of characters, 5ᵇ Mnemonic for the alphabet, 6ª–13ᵇ Text, 14ª–14ᵇ Table of combinations, 15ª–15ᵇ Text, 16ª Defectives of the first and second sorts, 16ᵇ Defectives of the third and fourth sorts, 17ª Defectives of the fifth and sixth sorts, 17ᵇ Defectives of the seventh and eighth sorts, 18ª Defectives of the ninth sort with additions, 18ᵇ Symbolicals, 19ª–22ª Text, 22ᵇ Colophon.

The only other copy of this edition recorded is in R.L.M. (Bailey coll., 514.L.69, wanting leaf A4), which also has the engraved title-page of the 10th edition, 1628, prefixed. The "Schoolmaster" is not found with it.

Copies of an earlier 12th edition, dated 1638 on the letterpress title-page but otherwise agreeing with the Pepysian copy, are in N.L.S. (Warden coll., Wn.877, wanting the "Schoolmaster") and C.L.W. (wanting the "Schoolmaster").

The 13th edition has a similar letterpress title-page, but the imprint reads: "*London*, | Printed by *Richard Cotes*, for *H.S.* and are | to be sold by

15

Richard Lownes, at his shop | without Ludgate. 1644." Colophon on last page: "*London*, | Printed by *Richard Cotes*, for *H.S.* and are | to be sold by *Richard Lowns*, at his shop | without *Ludgate*. 1644." The engraved title-page of the 10th edition, 1628, is prefixed. Copies are in the B.M.L. (Lewis coll., C.31.a.46.(2), wanting the "Schoolmaster"); R.L.M. (Bailey coll., 514.L.68, wanting the "Schoolmaster"); C.L.M. (Mun. D.1.85, Byrom coll., wanting A1, A2 and B8, wanting the "Schoolmaster"); C.L.E. (Pocknell coll., 570R 653, wanting the "Schoolmaster"); Munich University (English seminary); and the collection of Horace G. Healey, New York City (Trumbull coll., with the "Schoolmaster").

The 14th edition has a similar letterpress title-page, with a slight variation and a new imprint which reads: "London, | Printed for *Eliz. Purslow*, for *H.S.* and are | to be sold by *Richard Lownes*, at his shop | on Ludgate-hill. 1647." The colophon on the last page is also dated 1647. There are two copies of this edition in B.M.L. One of these (Fraser coll., 1043.a.65) has the engraved title-page of the 10th edition, 1628, prefixed; the other (7942.a.17) has a new engraved title-page bearing the imprint: "London Printed for Henry Seile over against St Dunstans Church in Fleet streete. 1648." Another copy of the 14th edition, with engraved title-page dated 1648, is in the Royal Library, Copenhagen.

On 15 December 1617 a Latin edition of the work was entered on the Stationers' Register to Robert Willis (Arber's *Transcript*, III, 617). *S.T.C.* 25747. The letterpress title reads as follows:

Stenographia, | *Siue ars* | Compendiosè Scribendi: rationem | ostendens, in linguæ Latinae ab- | *breuiatione omnes alias itidem* | *linguas contractiùs scribendi.* | Item, | Mnemonica | Siue | Reminiscendi Ars: è puris artis na- | turæque fontibus hausta, & | *in tres libros digesta.* | Nec non, | De Memoria natvra- | li fouenda libellus: è varijs do- | *ctissimorum operibus sedulò* | *collectus.* | Omnia iam primùm in lucem edita, auctore | Ioanne Willisso, sacræ | Theologiae bacchalaureo. | Omne bonum, Dei Donum. | *Vt vnaquæque ars nobilissima ac diuinissima* | *fuit: ità ad mortalium cognitionem tardissi-* | *mè peruenit.* Cardanus. | Londoni, | Per *Humfredum Lownes*, sumptibus | *Rob: Willis*; & *Nath: Browne.* 1618.

16

The latter part of this title is an exact reproduction of the title-page of Willis's work on memory printed in the same year. The only recorded copy is in B.L.O. (8° R.33.Art).

The | School-Master | to the Art of | Stenography. | Explaining the Rules, and teaching | the practise thereof, to the vnderstan- | ding of the meanest | capacity. | *Written by* | Iohn Willis, Batchelor in | Divinitie. | Allowed according to order. | *Rectum est sui index, &* *obliqui.* | The second Edition. | *London,* | Printed for *Henry Seyle,* and are to be sold at | the *Tygers-head* in St. *Pauls* Church- | yard. 1628. [402⁶.]

5⅝ × 3⅜ in., 16mo, pp. 100 letterpress with engraved folding "Table of Affixes". No numbers to pages. The running title is "The Schoolemaster to the Art of Stenographie". Sign. A–G3 in eights. Shorthand characters inserted in MS. *S.T.C.* 25751.

Leaf 1ᵃ Title, 1ᵇ blank, 2ᵃ–3ᵇ "To the Reader...Iohn Willis", 4ᵃ–40ᵇ Text, 41ᵃ Text contd., The exemplary sentences, 41ᵇ–50ᵃ The exemplary sentences contd., 50ᵇ Text concluded.

The Pepysian copy lacks the leaf G1 and the "Table of Affixes", which should follow B3. The spaces left for the insertion of the shorthand characters are blank in this copy.

Other copies are in B.M.L. (1043.a.63); B.L.O. (8° W.13.Art, bound with "The Art of Stenographie", 9th ed., 1628, wanting "Table of Affixes"); G.L.L. (C.8.6, with "Table of Affixes"); and the Henry E. Huntington Library, San Marino, California.

The first edition was entered on the Stationers' Register to Robert Willis on 13 November 1621 (Arber's *Transcript*, IV, 61). *S.T.C.* 25750. The only known copy is in U.L.C. (Syn.8.62.38). Its title reads:

The | *School-Maister* | to the Art of | Stenographie. | Explayning the Rules, and tea- | ching the practise thereof, to | the vnderstanding of the mea- | nest capacitie. | Written by | *Iohn Willis* Batcheler in | Diuinitie. | Allowed according to order. | *Rectum est sui index, & obliqui.* | [Ornament] | London |

Printed by *William Iones* for *Robert* | *Willis*, and are to be sould by *Hen.* | *Seile* at the Tigers head in | *Paules Church-yard.* | 1622.

24mo, pp. 100. No numbers to pages. Sign. A–H4 in twelves. E3 is wrongly lettered E5. On (H4) is printed: "These bookes are to be sold readie charactered or vncharactered by *Robert Willis*: who lodgeth at the house of Ms. Stubbes, dwelling in the alley, adioyning to Ludgate on the out side of the gate. And there also are to be sold Books of the Art of Stenographie, and of the Art of Memorie both in Latine and English."

The | School-Master | to the Art of | Stenography. | Explaining the Rules, and teaching | the practice thereof, to the understanding | of the meanest capacity. | Written heretofore by John Willis, | Bachelour in Divinity. | *The third Edition,* | Reviewed, perused, and exactly fitted | to the Art of Stenography of | the fourteenth Edition. | *Rectum est sui Index & Obliqui* | [Ornament] | London, | Printed by *R. L.* for *Henry Seile,* over against | St *Dunstans* Church in *Fleetstreet.* | MDCXLVII.   [402 13.]

5½ × 3¼ in., 16mo, pp. (6) + 90 letterpress with 1 engraved folding plate. The running title is "The Schoolmaster to the Art of Stenography". Sign. A–M4 in eights. Shorthand characters inserted in MS.

Leaf 1^a Title, 1^b blank, 2^a–3^b Epistle to the Reader...John Willis, 4^a–21^b Text, 22^a–24^b An Alphabeticall Table of the Words of Sort, 25^a–38^b Text, 39^a–48^b The Exemplary Sentences.

The only other recorded copy is in B.M.L. (7942.a.17, bound with "The Art of Stenography", 14th ed., 1647). A copy formerly in the Birmingham Free Library was destroyed by fire in 1880.

Another work by Willis consists of four small engraved pages, in double columns, with the title "Certaine Exemplary Sentences in Stenographicall Characters" along the top of the first two pages, and the date "Aug. 20, 1634" at the foot of the last page. The contents comprise the Lord's Prayer, the Creed, and a number of sentences in stenography. Copies are in B.M.L.

(7942.a.17, following the "Schoolmaster", 3rd ed., 1647) and N.L.S. (Warden coll., Wn.877, appended to "The Art of Stenographie", 12th ed., 1638).

In Willis's "School-Master", 2nd ed., 1628, and "The Art of Stenographie", 10th ed., 1632, reference is made to "The Singing Psalmes printed in a very small volume in stenographicall Characters". No copy of this book is known to be extant. The ninth edition of "The Art of Stenographie", 1628, does not mention "The Singing Psalmes".

To John Willis belongs the distinction of having invented the first stenographic alphabet capable of representing consecutively the sounds of any word in the English language, and of coining the name "stenography" which is still the most widely used designation for the art that owes so much to his pioneer labours. Willis's was the first system to provide for the expression of consonants, vowels and diphthongs by simple geometrical forms, and its basic principles were adopted by nearly all subsequent workers in this field during more than 200 years.

In his choice of material Willis aimed at allotting the shortest signs to the most frequent sounds and at facilitating the junction of those letters which occur most frequently in combination. A serious defect of his alphabet is that many of the signs were compound characters derived from the corresponding Hebrew, Greek and Roman capitals or the court and secretary hands of the period, only nine or ten being simple straight lines or curves. Any sign could be written either large or small, the larger size being reserved for initial letters. Initial vowels were indicated, like the consonants, by alphabetic signs, final vowels by a disjoined dot or dash in proximity to the preceding consonant. Medial vowels were shown by the ingenious device of varying the position of the consonants in relation to each other to indicate the intervening vowel. For this purpose each of the five vowels was allotted a definite place above, below, or on either side of the consonant.

The phonetic principle to which most English shorthand inventors have attached so much importance was recognised by Willis when he wrote: "In this Art, not the Orthographie, but the sound of the word is respected." And again: "In every word, those letters are to be omitted, which are but lightly, or not at all sounded, whether they be vowels or consonants." Arbitrary signs were provided for a number of double and treble consonants, and special rules laid down for the abbreviation of words and sentences. Willis gave at some length his reasons for writing from left to right "and not from the toppe to the bottome of the leafe as the inhabitantes of China are reported to doe" and as Timothy Bright had done.

Willis's shorthand was the first to be introduced into Germany, Georg Philipp Harsdörffer having reproduced his alphabet in the third part of Schwenter's "Deliciæ Philosophicæ et Mathematicæ" (Nuremberg, 1653). A detailed description of the system was given by Dr Christian Johnen in *Archiv für Stenographie*, Berlin, vol. LIX (1908). The fullest accounts in English are to be found in Edward Pocknell's "Origin of Modern Shorthand Characters" (reprinted from *Shorthand*, II, 50–1, 1883); "A Critical and Historical Account of the Art of Shorthand", by Hugh W. Innes & George Carl Mares, in *The National Stenographer*, Chicago, III, 17–19, 1892; and "Three Centuries of Alphabetic Shorthand", by Alexander Paterson, in *The Phonetic Journal*, LXI, 6–7, 1902.

JOHN WILLIS (1572?–1625) graduated B.A. at Christ's College, Cambridge, in 1592, took his M.A. degree four years later, and in 1603 became S.T.B., the equivalent of the modern B.D. Nothing more is known of his early career, though some passages in his works suggest that he had studied the law to some purpose. On 12 June 1601 Willis was presented by the Dean and Chapter of Canterbury to the rectory of St Mary Bothaw, Dowgate Hill, London, the site of which is now covered by Cannon Street railway station. His daughter Elizabeth was baptised in the parish church on 24 January 1601/2. Three months later "The Art of Stenographie" was entered on the Stationers' Register to the publisher, Cuthbert Burby, who was one of Willis's parishioners. No indication of the author's name was given in the register or in the book, but later editions show that it was from the pen of John Willis, whose identity was not disclosed probably for reasons not unconnected with the unexpired "privilege" granted by Elizabeth to Dr Timothy Bright fourteen years previously (see p. 4).

In 1603 London was ravaged by the plague and Willis lost three of his children in quick succession—Richard, buried at St Mary Bothaw on 28 June;

John, who died of the plague in the following October; Elizabeth, buried 10 December. This triple bereavement must have been a heavy blow and may have led him to leave the plague-stricken city and seek a rural retreat. On 1 July 1606 he was presented to the rectory of Bentley Parva, near Colchester, then in the gift of Paul and Andrew Bayning, aldermen of London. Here another daughter was christened Elizabeth in the following September, and a daughter Martha, baptised on 20 April 1610, was buried the next day.

The fifth edition of "The Art of Stenographie", printed in 1617 by William White, the printer of the first edition, bore the author's and printer's names on the title-page. It was entered on the Stationers' Register to Robert Willis, whose name appears at the end of the book as a teacher of stenography, lodging "at the house of M. Dauies without Ludgate". He was doubtless the Robert Willis, son of John Willis of London, clerk, who was entered as a scholar at the Merchant Taylors' School in 1605 and admitted a freeman of the Stationers' Company on 9 October 1617.

John Willis's "Mnemonica, siue reminiscendi ars" was entered on the register a few days later, also to Robert Willis, but the extant copies are dated 1618. An English version of the third part of this work was printed in 1621 with the title "The Art of Memory", and a later edition appeared in 1654. The first complete translation of the Latin original was made by Leonard Sowersby and published by him in 1661[1]. A Latin version of Willis's shorthand entitled "Stenographia", entered to his son Robert in December 1617, was published in the following year. In November 1621 "The Schoolemaster to the Arte of Stenography" was entered to Robert Willis, who was then living "at the house of Ms. Stubbes, dwelling in the alley adioyning to Ludgate on the out side of the gate", but soon afterwards joined his father at Little Bentley and was buried there on 13 September 1622. The entry in the parish register reveals that his mother's name was Sara.

John Willis saw some further editions of his stenography through the press and, conscious perhaps that his end was approaching, wrote in the eighth edition, 1623: "I haue thought good, after so many severall Editions of this Art, now to set the last hand thereunto, with purpose neuer to alter it hereafter." On 28 November 1625 he was buried in the church of Little Bentley, where he had ministered for nearly twenty years.

[1] A copy is in the Pepysian Library, No. 310.

The 300th anniversary of the publication of Willis's stenography was commemorated in 1902 by the foundation of the Willis-Byrom Club, an Anglo-American association of shorthand enthusiasts, with the object of keeping alive and stimulating an interest in the history and literature of the art.
(A. T. Wright's *John Willis, S.T.B. and Edmond Willis*, 1926.)

An | Abbreviation | of VVriting by | Character. | Wherein is summarily contained, | *A Table, which is an Abstract of* | the whole Art. | With | *Plaine and easie Rules for the speedy per-* | formance thereof, without any | other *Tutor.* | By *Edmond Willis.* | The Second Edition, much enlarged, for the | full satisfying of what hath beene desired. | [Ornament] | *London:* | Printed by *George Purslowe*, and are to bee sold by | *Nicholas Bourne*, at the South doore of the *Royall* | *Exchange:* and by *Philemon Stephens*, at the | *Golden Lyon* in *Pauls* Churchyard. | 1627.   [860¹².]

6½ × 4¼ in., 8vo, pp. (9) + 22 + (8) letterpress, and 8 engraved leaves printed on one side. With headlines. Sign. A–C4 in eights. Colophon on recto of last leaf: "Printed by *George Purslowe*. 1627". Title within double-ruled border. Shorthand characters in the text in MS. (red ink). *S.T.C.* 25742. Prefixed is an engraved title-page within a framework of emblematical figures, by Francis Delaram (Johnson, No. 2), which reads as follows:

An | Abreuiation of Writing by | Character | *Wherein is summarily conteyned* | *a Table which is an Ab=* | *stract of ỹ whole Art* | *With plaine &* | *easie Rules for the* | *speedie performance thereof* | *without any other Tutor.* | By *Edmond Willis* | All that thine hand shall finde to doe, | doe it quicklie for there is neither Art, | Invention, knowledge nor Wisdome | in ỹ graue whither thou goest Eccle. 9. 10 | *The same by Character* | [Two lines of shorthand characters.] | The second edition, much enlargd, | for the full satisfying of what hath bēn desired. | London: | *Printed by George Purslowe,* *and are to* | *be sould by Nicholas Bourne, at the South* | *doore of the Royall* *Exchange: and by* | *Philemon Stephens, at the golden* | *Lyon in Pauls church-* *yard.* | Anno 1627.

Leaf 1ᵃ Engraved title, 1ᵇ blank, 2ᵃ Letterpress title, 2ᵇ blank, 3ᵃ–6ᵃ The Preface to the Reader...Edmond Willis, 6ᵇ–7ᵃ blank, 7ᵇ–8ᵃ The Table, containing alphabet, double consonants, vowels' places, terminations and prepositions, 8ᵇ–9ᵃ blank, 9ᵇ–10ᵃ Terminations for long words, 10ᵇ blank, 11ᵃ–15ᵇ Text, 16ᵃ Examples, 16ᵇ blank, 17ᵃ–19ᵇ Text, 20ᵃ Examples, 20ᵇ blank, 21ᵃ–21ᵇ Text, 22ᵃ blank, 22ᵇ–23ᵃ 200 usuall words and particles, 23ᵇ blank, 24ᵃ–25ᵇ Text, 26ᵃ–29ᵃ Table for words of many syllables, 29ᵇ Verses "In laudem Authoris" by M. Billingsley.

B.M.L. (2 copies, 7942.aa.37 and 1043.b.60, the latter wanting engraved title-page); B.L.O. (8° M.24.Linc.); C.L.M. (Byrom coll., 2.K.5.33, wanting 2 plates); R.L.M. (Bailey coll., 514.L.70, wanting 3 plates); M.L.W. (2827); S.L.D. (C.a.2); U.L.Y. (Healey coll., F.25.136). W.J.C. John Byrom records that his copy, with three other books, cost him 1s. 2d. on 16 March 1725 (*Journal*, I, 96).

The first edition of Edmond Willis's shorthand treatise was published in 1618, and was entered on the Stationers' Register to George Purslowe on 28 June of that year (Arber's *Transcript*, III, 628). *S.T.C.* 25741. It bore a similar engraved title to that of the second edition, the imprint being replaced by a landscape within an oval cartouche inscribed "Ex fonte flumina." There is no letterpress title and the colophon on the last page reads: "Printed by *George Purslow*, 1618." Two distinct issues of this edition are known. The first contains a dedication to Nicholas, Lord Bishop of Coventry and Lichfield. The only recorded copy is in B.M.L. (C.31.b.12). The second issue is dedicated to Nicholas, Lord Bishop of Bristoll, and the re-engraved title-page shows some slight variations. Copies of this issue are in B.L.O. (8° W.13.Art) and L.C.W. (Z56.W734).

Edmond Willis's outstanding contribution to shorthand progress was the construction of a shorthand alphabet in which simple straight lines and curves predominated. Only four of John Willis's characters, those for *o*, *v*, *w* and *z*, were retained in his system, and the number of compound signs was reduced by nearly one half, all the rectangles and semi-ellipses of his predecessor being discarded in favour of simpler and more facile forms. While adopting his namesake's method of vocalisation in the main, he rejected the plan of writing a single vowel on the left side of a consonant, realising that this would involve many retrograde movements of the pen, and reserved the left side for the less frequent double vowels and diphthongs. As Dr John R. Gregg has pointed out ("The Story of Shorthand", in *The Business Education World*, xv, 184, 1934), only two of Edmond Willis's characters necessitated a back-slope movement of the pen, and practically all of them could be written on the slope of longhand without risk to legibility. Other noteworthy features of the system are the provision of alternative signs for five letters, the introduction of looped characters (*p* and *q*) which were employed much more extensively and effectively in the eighteenth century, notably by Byrom and Taylor, and a useful list of prepositions and terminations.

Edmond Willis's system bears the impress of the practical shorthand writer, as opposed to the mere theoretician, and its most original features are almost certainly the outcome of experience in actual note-taking.

EDMOND WILLIS (1575–16—), son of Thomas Willis, draper of Salisbury, was baptised on 2 March 1574/5 at St Thomas's, Salisbury. In June 1592 he was apprenticed for eight years to Thomas Hooper, merchant tailor of Bow Lane, London, and was made free of the Merchant Taylors Company on 24 November 1600. On 18 February 1602/3 a licence was issued for the marriage of Edmund Willis, of St Thomas-the-Apostle, merchant tailor, to Dorothy Talbot, of St Mary Magdalen, Milk Street, spinster, daughter of Stephen Talbot, of Salisbury, haberdasher (J. Foster's *London Marriage Licences, 1521–1869*, 1887, col. 1479). The marriage took place on the following 6 March at St Mary Magdalen. Willis's son Nathaniel, born on 3 January 1605, was admitted to the Merchant Taylors' School in 1614 (C. J. Robinson's *Register*, 1882, I, 81), and is perhaps the Nathaniel Willis who took up his freedom in the Stationers' Company on 7 December 1635 (Arber's *Transcript*, III, 688). Another son, Ephraim, baptised at St Antholin's, Budge Row, on 26 September 1609, was buried on 16 December following; while a daughter Elizabeth was baptised on 10 January 1612/13, and another daughter Ann was buried on 17 March 1617/18.

Willis must have taken up the study of shorthand soon after his marriage, perhaps as a result of the publication by his namesake, John Willis, of a treatise on the subject in 1602 (see p. 13). In his "Abbreviation of the Art of Writing by Character", 1618, he wrote: "Such hath beene my labour and earnest desire for these fourteene yeeres past, to attaine to some perfection in this Art, that I haue not failed to seeke to all men, that haue made any profession of teaching the same in this Citie. Besides, I thinke I haue written as much with mine own hand in that kind, as any man in this Cittie." In dedicating his book to Nicholas Felton, Bishop of Bristol, he specified that he had taken down Felton's sermons "by the space of many yeeres". Felton was for 28 years rector of St Antholin's, in which parish Willis had been living, and was rector of St Mary-le-Bow, Cheapside, from 1596 until he became Bishop of Bristol in 1617. A MS. volume in the Carlton collection has for its title: "Certaine Sermons godley & Learnedley preached By Mr Nicholas Felton Doctor of Diuinitie And Taken from his mouth. . . . London Anno Domini 1606." The sermons are eight in number and are in longhand. The first was preached at "St Antlins" on 5 August 1599, the others at "Bowe, Chepeside", the latest on 13 January 1605/6.

One of the reasons given by Willis for not inviting pupils to repair to him for further instruction in the art was that he considered his book to contain everything necessary for the learner, and he added: "I praise God I haue another calling, wherein God hath placed mee, and to which I doe apply my self, hauing therby (through Gods blessing) sufficient means." From this it may be inferred that his occupation of merchant tailor was a fairly lucrative one. The statement in the second edition of his shorthand treatise, published in 1627, that he had found "much gaine and benefit" by taking sermons and speeches verbatim was quoted by Matthias Levy (*History of Short-Hand Writing*, 1862, p. 27) as evidence that Willis was one of the earliest professional shorthand writers; but this interpretation does not seem compatible with the repeated reference to "my other Calling wherto I giue attendance" and which "doth furnish me with an Estate sufficiently sutable to the moderation of my desires". The first edition contains verses in praise of the author from the pens of Nicholas Breton and Martin Billingsley, the famous writing master who was Willis's neighbour in Bush Lane near London Stone.

The date and place of Edmond Willis's death have not been ascertained. J. H. Lewis (*Historical Account of the Rise and Progress of Short Hand*, 1816, p. 58) observes that Willis was "a man of talents and learning; and, as far as can be deduced from his own language, of exemplary piety". He expressly disclaimed any pretension to learning, however, and modestly confessed himself "but a meane scholler in comparison of others".

(A. T. Wright's *John Willis, S.T.B. and Edmond Willis*, 1926.)

25

Brachygraphie, Post-Writt. | Or, | The Art | of | *Short-writing* | Where most Letters consist of sin- | -gle stroakes or motions of the Pen, | in best formes of Penship. | *The practise is speedy and pleasant,* *bet-* | *-ters the hand for hands of best approued* | *vse, and is accommodated* *for all Lan-* | *-guages expressible by spelling.* | *The second Edition.* | Much refined and enlarged, teaching, by | the verball Part onely, a speedy dispatch | in taking of speeches, by any meane | vulgar hands. | *Per* G. Folkingham G. | *London,* | Printed by *Thomas Snodham.* | 1622. [402⁸.]

$5\frac{5}{8} \times 3\frac{1}{2}$ in., 8vo, pp. (12) + 26 letterpress, engraved folding plate of alphabet, etc., and a folding leaf of letterpress between pp. 18, 19, containing "Spurs for Post-Writt". With headlines. Sign. A–A6, B–B8, C–C4, D1.

Leaf 1ᵃ Title, 1ᵇ blank, 2ᵃ–4ᵃ To the Reader, 4ᵇ–5ᵇ Verses "To the Masters of the Post, t'all Postagers", etc., 6ᵃ Verses by Thomas Bonham, 6ᵇ Verses by Martin Billingsley, 7ᵃ–19ᵇ "Post-Writt".

The Pepysian copy is one of two known copies of this edition. The other, which is in the Duke of Devonshire's library at Chatsworth, contains on the back of the engraved plate a written inscription to Lord Cavendish with Folkingham's signature dated 19 September 1622.

The first edition was entered on the Stationers' Register to Thomas Snodham on 10 July 1620 (Arber's *Transcript*, IV, 39). *S.T.C.* 11122. The only copy recorded is in B.L.O. (8° S.106.Art), its full title being: "*Brachigraphy, Post-writ,* | or, | The Art | of | *Short-writing.* | The Summe whereof is couch- | ed into one Table, plainely demon- | strating the whole Method of the | Invention. | *By* W. Folkingham his Maie- | sties *Post* of *Stamford.* | [Ornament] | London: | Printed by *Thomas Snodham*". This edition consists of 12 leaves (Sign. A–A8, B–B4). The table referred to in the title is lacking from the Bodleian copy.

On 23 February 1625–6 Snodham's widow assigned her rights in the "Arte of Brachygraphye..." to William Stansby (Arber's *Transcript*, IV, 152), but no edition is known to have been published by him.

26

Further details of both editions and a typographical reproduction of a portion of the second edition will be found in Alexander Tremaine Wright's "William Folkingham: Mathesios et Medicinæ studiosus", 1898.

Although it has received scant attention from most historians of shorthand, Folkingham's brachygraphy is one of the few original systems of the seventeenth century, and marks a great advance on those that preceded it. It contains the germ of the modern cursive or script stenographies. The author's declared aim was "the husbanding of the hand (as of time and place) that it might not with distorted characts be discustomed from good forms of usual letters". The alphabet was composed in part from selected portions of the ordinary longhand letters, very few of the signs being borrowed from earlier systems. Folkingham laid down the following axiom for the construction of a shorthand alphabet: "That Characts may briefly be impressed they must in particular consist of single or concrete motions of the penne, and be limited respectively to several letters of the Alphabet, that they may aptly incorporate into double consonants and other couplings." His own alphabet is divided into three groups, "according to the several scite and analogie they hold with the supposed Line or Rule you write by". Not only was he the first to advocate writing in position, but he seems to have anticipated the "blended consonants" of some modern cursive systems, many of the consonantal combinations being obtained by simple junction ("a self-lineall and immediate continuation of the Stroake, where imagination, rather than sensible distinction or connection, limits th' extension and latitude of each severall Letter therein comprised").

For the representation of vowels Folkingham relied chiefly on implication by position. To each of the five vowels, *a, e, i, o, u,* a position was allotted in relation to an imaginary "diapent" or fivefold division by parallel lines, "cutting long-wayes through the breadth of the Letters or Line". Intermediate vowels could be indicated by contiguity of the preceding and following consonants—the so-called "vowel mode" introduced by John Willis. But the most original feature of Folkingham's plan of vowel indication was the writing of the consonants in sequence, without disjoining, the point of junction showing which vowel was to be read. "The peculiar implication of vowels in this Method is attributed to the immediate laterall

27

and single touch of consonants in Vowell regions." The system is refreshingly free from the arbitrary symbols so much in favour with the majority of shorthand "inventors" of this period.

The reasons for the neglect of this early shorthand author by writers on the history of the art are twofold. The first is the extreme rarity of Folkingham's book; the second lies in the ambiguity of his language, which abounds in quaint turns of expression and neologisms (many of them drawn from the terminology of music), and is occasionally so fantastic as to render his meaning obscure.

WILLIAM FOLKINGHAM (1575–1629) belonged to a family which took its name from the small Lincolnshire town of Folkingham or Falkingham. One of three sons of Edmund Folkingham of Helpringham, a village near Folkingham, he was baptised on 15 January 1575 at Helpringham, and was apparently living there when he wrote his first book: "Feudigraphia: The Synopsis or Epitome of Surveying methodized." It was published in London with a dedication to William Lord Compton, afterwards Earl of Northampton, dated 6 June 1610. On 4 December 1613 he was married at Helpringham to Anne Newlove, of that parish, a widow. For some years after this he appears to have been the tenant of Exeter Inn, Stamford, and on 10 January 1615 was admitted to the freedom of the borough of Stamford. In 1620 he is found installed as postmaster of that town, his emoluments consisting of 2s. a day. Folkingham was in the enjoyment of this office when his shorthand textbook was published, and a perusal of it shows that the range of his studies embraced mathematics, medicine and music. His tenure of the postmastership was probably of short duration, as the reference to "his Maiesties Post of Stamford" on the title-page of the 1620 edition is omitted from that of the edition printed two years later. The book abounds in postal metaphors redolent of the king's highway, and the second edition is divided into "postages" and "stages".

His next work, printed in 1623, was entitled "Panala, ala catholica, or A compound Ale: which is a generall Pvrge and generous Medicin for most infirmities incident to the Bodie of Man". The author is described as "Guil: Folkingham, Gen: Mathesios et Medicinæ Studiosus". He praises the virtue of ale as a wholesome beverage, and announces the discovery of a medicine composed of a preparation of herbs steeped in ale which Folkingham considered as a sovereign remedy for most of the ills that flesh is heir to and particularly as a preservative against epidemics. These herbs were to be had in bags or "funds" at the price of five shillings "with purgers", or half the money without. A second and enlarged edition of the book appeared in 1628 with the title: "Panala medica; vel sanitatis et longævitatis Alumna Catholica: The fruitfull and frugall Nourse of sound Health and long Life". In January of the following year Folkingham died and was buried in St Martin's Church, Stamford Baron, to the poor of which parish he bequeathed forty shillings, in addition to bequests of money to his brothers John and Thomas, with remainder to his widow and executrix.

(A. T. Wright's *William Folkingham: Mathesios et Medicinæ Studiosus*, 1898, and *Addenda*, 1906.)

Tachygraphy. | The most | Exact and Compendious | Method of Short and Swift | Writing, that hath ever yet | been Published by any. | Composed by | *Thomas Shelton*, | Author and Professor of | of the said Art. | Approved by both the | Universities. | *London* | Printed by *Thomas Milbourn*, for *Dorman* | *Newman* at the *Kings Arms* in the | Poultry, 1691. [860¹⁰.]

The above is the letterpress title. Prefixed is an engraved title as follows:

Tachygraphy | or | Short-Writing | The | most easie | exact and | speedie | First | Composed | by | Thomas Shelton | and | now by him Newly | Corrected & | Enlarged

$6\frac{3}{8} \times 3\frac{7}{8}$ in., 8vo, pp. (12)+44 letterpress and engraved. Title within border of printer's ornaments. Sign. A–D4 in eights. The running title is "The Art of Short-Writing".

Leaf 1ᵃ Engraved title, 1ᵇ blank, 2ᵃ letterpress title, 2ᵇ blank, 3ᵃ–3ᵇ Dedication "To the Worshipful his very Worthy Friend, Richard Knightely Esq;... Tho. Shelton", 4ᵃ–4ᵇ To the reader, 5ᵃ–6ᵃ Verses to the author, 6ᵇ The letters of the Alphabet, 7ᵃ–7ᵇ Text, 8ᵃ Double Consonants, 8ᵇ–12ᵇ Text, 13ᵃ Prepositions for longe words, Terminations for longe words, 13ᵇ–17ᵃ Text, 17ᵇ Markes for the Names of the bookes of the old and New Testament, 18ª Examples, 18ᵇ blank, 19ª Examples, 19ᵇ–21ᵇ Text, 22ª The table, 22ᵇ blank, 23ª The table, 23ᵇ blank, 24ª The table, 24ᵇ blank, 25ª The table, 25ᵇ–28ª Text Finis, 28ᵇ Arms and crest above the Lord's Prayer, the Creed and the Ten Commandments in shorthand.

This, which Pepys calls "the last of numerous editions", is a reissue of an earlier edition, with the old engraved title-page from which the imprint and date have been erased, and with a new letterpress title-page. The imprint, imperfectly obliterated, appears to have been: "*London, printed for M. Simmons dwelling next door to the Golden Lion in Aldersgate street.*" The Pepysian copy has only five preliminary leaves, the first leaf after the letter-press title being A3. Other copies are in B.M.L. (G.16758.(3)); N.L.S. (Warden coll., Wn.870); L.N.Y. (Howard coll., Reserve), and W.J.C.

Shelton's first work on shorthand was entered on the Stationers' Register to Samuel Cartwright on 17 April 1626 as "A booke Called Shorte writinge by Thomas Shelton" (Arber's *Transcript*, IV, 159). No copy of the first edition is known to be extant. The second edition, of which there are copies in B.L.O. (Mason AA.67.(2)), P.L.L. and W.J.C. (frontispiece and title-page in facsimile), bore the following title: "Short=writing | *The* | *most exact methode* | *By* | *Thomas Shelton* |*Author and Professor of ẙ said art.* | *The second edition inlarged. Printed by I: D: for S: C: & are to be sould at the Professors house in Cheapeside, over against Bowe Church....*1630." The Bodleian copy contains an engraved frontispiece by Robert Vaughan. The printer was John Dawson. *S.T.C.* 22404.

Shelton's "Tachygraphy" was entered on the London Stationers' Register to Samuel Cartwright on 9 February 1637–8 (Arber's *Transcript*, IV, 408), but an edition was printed at Cambridge as early as 1635. The only known copy is in the Carlton collection. The engraved title-page prefixed to this edition reads: "Tachy graphy | *The* | *Most exact and compendious* | *methode of short and swift* | *writing that hath euer yet* | *beene published by any* | *Composed by.* | Thomas Shelton | *Author and professor of the* | *said Art.* | *Approoued by both Vnyuersities,* | *printed by the printers to the Vniuersitie of* Cambridg | *for I. H. and are sold at* | *the professors house in Cheapside ouer against* | Bow-Chvrch." This title occupies the cover space within a border representing the outlines of a book. The volume consists of 8 + 29 letterpress pages, an engraved frontispiece of arms surmounting the Lord's prayer, Creed and Ten Commandments, engraved title-page and 10 other engraved plates. The date 1635 is on the last page of letterpress which is printed in red, the shorthand characters in the text being inserted in red ink.

The earliest edition with a London imprint which has been located has a similar engraved "book" title-page prefixed, with the following imprint: "London *Printed for* Samuel Cartwright *and are to be soulde at the hand and Bible in duck-Lane* 1639. *Ralph Hall* sculptor." The colophon on the last page of letterpress is dated 1639, and below is printed: "Feb. 9. 1637. Imprimatur Tho. Wykes". The date 1639 also appears at the foot of the last engraved page, containing Shelton's arms above the Lord's prayer, the Creed and the Ten Commandments in shorthand. The volume consists of the engraved title-page, (8) + 30 letterpress pages and 9 engraved plates. The only known copy of this edition is in B.L.M. It apparently lacks two plates.

Another edition in R.L.M. (Bailey coll., 514.K.71) has a slightly different colophon, dated 1639, on the last page of letterpress, followed by: "Feb. 9. 1637. Imprimatur Tho. Wykes.", and exhibits other differences in the text. Prefixed is the engraved "book" title-page of Ralph Hall with the same imprint, followed by the date 1641.

Another edition has the engraved "book" title-page of Ralph Hall prefixed, but the imprint reads: "*printed by the printer to the Vniversitie of* Cambridg R D *and are sold at the professors house in Old Fish-streete neare Bread-streetehill*. . . . *Ralph Hall sculptor* 1641". The printer was Roger Daniel. There is no colophon or date inside. Copies are in B.G.P. (Guénin coll., Δ 68365), C.L.E. (Pocknell coll., 508R/653, lacking title-page), and L.N.Y. (Beale coll., Reserve).

Another edition, with the same engraved "book" title-page of Ralph Hall, dated 1641, has the date 1641 at the foot of the last engraved page, but the colophon on the last page of letterpress is dated 1642. Copies of this edition are in B.L.O. (Ashm.E.15.(4)) and W.J.C.

Another edition, of which a copy is in B.M.L. (C.31.a.46.(3)), has the same engraved "book" title-page of Ralph Hall, dated 1641, but the colophon on the last page of letterpress is slightly different from the preceding and is dated 1644.

There is no record of an edition of "Tachygraphy" containing a letterpress title of earlier date than 1645. The letterpress title of one edition reads: "Tachy-graphy. The Most exact and compendious methode of short and swift writing that hath ever yet been published by any. *Composed by* Thomas Shelton Authour and Professour of the said Art. *Approved by both the Universities, and are to be sold at the Professours house in the* Poultrey *near the Church. Anno Dom.* 1645." Prefixed is an engraved title-page by Thomas Cross (Johnson, No. 3), representing a flaming heart surmounting an architectural design, within which is the title: "Tachygraphy or short-writing *The* most easie exact and speedie *First Composed by Thomas Shelton and now by him Newly Corrected & Enlarged* 1645 *Printed at Cambridg by R: D: And are sold at the Authors house Crosse sculp.*" The book consists of (8) + 52 pp. in addition to the title-pages. Copies are in B.M.L. (11632.a.47(4)); N.L.S. (Warden coll., Wn.865); University Library, St Andrews; C.L.W. (Walford coll.); L.N.Y. (Howard coll., Reserve); and C.E.B. (Havette coll.).

Another edition has a similar letterpress title-page with the imprint: "Printed at *London* by R. C. for *Samuel Cartwright*, and are to be sold at the hand and Bible in *Duck-lane.* 1645." The printer was Richard Cotes. This consists of (10) + 44 pp. A copy is in B.M.L. (C.31.a.49.(1)).

Another edition has a similar letterpress title-page with the date 1646. A copy in W.J.C. has the letterpress colophon on p. 43: "Printed at *London* by *Richard Cotes* for *Samuel Cartwright*, and are to bee sold at the hand and Bible in *Ducklane*, 1645." At the foot of the last (engraved) page is: "*London Printed for Samuel Cartwright and are to be Soulde at the hand and Bible in duck-lane*, 1647." The engraved title-page of 1645 by Cross is prefixed, but the date and imprint have been altered to read: "1647 *London Printed for Sa: Cartwright & are to be sould at the Hand & Bible in Duck-lane.*" An engraved portrait of Shelton, aet. 46, is prefixed to the Carlton copy. Another copy, without the portrait and the engraved title-page, is in L.C.W. (Z56.S545).

Another edition has a similar letterpress title-page with the imprint: "Printed by *Roger Daniel*, Printer to the Universitie of *Cambridge*. 1647." The engraved title-page of 1645 by Cross is prefixed, but in some copies the date and imprint have been removed from the plate. There is no colophon. Copies are in the U.L.C. (L.32.57²); S.L.D.; L.N.Y. (Heffley coll., *IDE, wanting engraved title-page and pp. 19–20, 49–51); N.L.S. (Warden coll., Wn.866); and W.J.C. (H. B. Wheatley's copy, with his "Bibliotheca Pepysiana Secunda" bookplate and anchor device stamped in gilt on sides).

On 25 January 1649/50 Samuel Cartwright and Matthew Simmons were entered on the Stationers' Register as holders of the copyright of "Tachygraphy", as well as of Shelton's "Tutor" and "Zeiglographia" (Roxb. *Transcript*, I, 336). Cartwright died on 17 August 1650 and Matthew Simmons on 19 May 1654. On 19 April 1659 Cartwright's half-share in the copyright of the three books was assigned to Mrs Mary Simmons, Matthew's widow (Roxb. *Transcript*, II, 222). An edition of "Tachygraphy" was issued with a letterpress title-page bearing the imprint: "*London*; Printed by *M. Simmons*, dwelling next doore to the Golden Lyon in Aldersgate streete, 1660." There is an undated letterpress colophon at the foot of p. 43, and at the foot of the last (engraved) page is: "London Printed by M: Simmons: and are to be Soulde next dore to the Golden Lion in Aldersgate street 1660." Prefixed is the engraved title-page by Cross with the date 1659 followed by the imprint: "London Printed by M: Simmons in Aldersgate Street, next doore to the Golden Lion." Copies are in B.L.O. (25788.f.129) and W.J.C. A copy in U.L.C. (M.18.92) agrees in every respect save that the last (engraved) page has at the foot: "London Printed for Samuel Cartwright and are to be Soulde at the hand and Bible in duck-lane, 1647."

Another edition has a similar letterpress title-page with the imprint: "*London*, Printed by *M. Simmons*, dwelling next door to the Golden Lyon in *Aldersgate Street*, 1668." Prefixed is the engraved title-page by Cross dated 1645. A copy is in W.J.C. Another edition has a similar letterpress title-page with the imprint: "*London*, Printed by *S. Simmons*, dwelling next door to the Golden Lion in *Aldersgate Street*, 1671." The letterpress colophon on p. 43 reads: "Printed at *London* for *S. Simmons*, dwelling next door to the Golden *Lyon* in *Aldersgate street*", and at the foot of the last (engraved) page is: "*London Printed by M: Simmons: and are to be Soulde next dore to the Golden Lion in Aldersgate street 1671*". Prefixed is the engraved title-page by Cross with the imprint: "*London printed for M Simmons, next door to the golden lion in Aldersgate street. 1671.*" The printer, Samuel Simmons, was presumably the son of Matthew and Mary. This may be the edition announced in the Term Catalogue, Hilary 1671–2, as "Printed for M. Simmons, and are to be sold by the several Booksellers of London. 1s." (*T.C.* 1, 99). Copies are in B.M.L. (787.a.74.(1), 1043.b.59 and 1043.a.54 (wanting engraved title-page)); G.L.L. (C.8.4, wanting letterpress title-page); R.L.M. (Bailey coll., 514.K.74, with the date 1660 on the last page); C.L.W. (Fraser and Walford colls.); Sir F. Newdegate's library, Arbury, Nuneaton; Bibliothèque Nationale, Paris (V.25094); B.L.M. (wanting both title-pages); L.N.Y. (Howard coll., Reserve); the Public Library, Brooklyn, N.Y. (6431.10); U.L.Y. (Healey coll., F25.154); and W.J.C. (O'Donnell coll., incomplete).

Another edition has a similar letterpress title-page dated 1674. The letterpress colophon on p. 43 is undated, and the engraved colophon has been removed from the foot of the last page. Prefixed is the engraved title-page by Cross, with the imprint: "*London Printed for M Simmons, next door to the Golden Lion in Aldersgate street*, 1671". This edition was announced in the Term Catalogue, Michaelmas 1674, as "Printed by S. Simmons, and sold by P. Parker at the Leg and Star in Cornhill. Price, stitcht, 1s." (*T.C.* 1, 192). Copies are in L.P.L. (47.E.3); M.L.W. (39.J.15); P.L.L.; B.L.M.; Mercantile Library, Philadelphia; J.R.G.; and W.J.C.

Another edition has a similar letterpress title-page with the imprint: "*London*, Printed by *T. M.* for *D. Newman* at the *Kings Arms* in the *Poultry*, *T. Passenger* at the *Three Bibles* on *London-Bridge*, and *T. Sawbridge*, at the *Flower-de-Luce* in *Little-Britain*, 1685." Prefixed is the engraved title-page by Cross from which the imprint has been removed. This edition was announced as "reprinted" in the Term Catalogue, Hilary 1685

34

(*T.C.* ii, 119). Copies are in R.L.M. (Bailey coll., 514.K.76), Birmingham Reference Library, and S.L.D. (C.a.3ª).

Another reprint was announced in the Term Catalogue, Trinity 1687, as "printed for D. Newman at King's Arms in the Poultrey" (*T.C.* ii, 203). No copy with this date has been located.

Another reprint was announced in the Term Catalogue, Easter 1689, as "sold by T. Speed at the Crown in the Poultrey" (*T.C.* ii, 263). No copy with this date has been located.

Another reprint was announced in the Term Catalogue, Michaelmas 1690, as "printed for T. Speed at the Three Crowns in Cornhill" (*T.C.* ii, 341). No copy with this date or imprint has been located.

Another reprint was announced in the Term Catalogue, Michaelmas 1692 (*T.C.* ii, 430). No copy with this date has been located.

Another edition has a letterpress title-page similar to that of the 1691 edition, with the imprint: "*London*, Printed by *Thomas Milbourn*, for *Dorman Newman* at the *King's Arms* in the *Poultrey*, 1693." Prefixed is the engraved title-page by Cross with the imprint: "*London Printed for Dorman Newman at the King's Armes, in the Poultry*, 1693." There is no colophon. This is perhaps the reprint announced in the Term Catalogue, Hilary 1693, as "printed for Tho. Speed at the Three Crowns in Cornhill" (*T.C.* ii, 444). Copies are in B.M.L. (1042.b.48); R.L.M. (Bailey coll., 514.K.77); C.L.W. (Walford coll.); L.N.Y. (Beale coll., *IDS p.v.73, no. 5); and W.J.C.

Another edition has a similar letterpress title-page with the imprint: "*London* Printed, and are to be Sold by the Booksellers of *London* and *Westminster*." Prefixed is the engraved title-page by Cross from which the imprint has been removed and "Price 1.ˢʰⁱˡˡ" substituted. "Corrected" is misspelled "Coreceted". This edition was announced in the Term Catalogue, Michaelmas 1706, as "printed for the Booksellers of London and Westminster" (*T.C.* iii, 528). Copies are in B.M.L. (C.31.a.47); R.L.M. (Bailey coll., 514.K.80); C.L.M. (Mun.D.2.2); P.L.L.; C.L.W. (Walford coll., wanting engraved title-page); S.L.D. (C.a.3ᵃ); and the collections of R. H. G. Smallwood, Gresford, Wrexham, and W.J.C.

The last recorded edition of "Tachygraphy" has a similar letterpress title-page with the imprint: "*London*, Printed for *E. Tracy*, at the Three *Bibles*, on *London-Bridge*. 1710." Prefixed is the engraved title-page by Cross from which the imprint and part of the date have been obliterated. There is no colophon. This edition was announced in the Term Catalogue, Easter 1711, as "printed for E. Tracy at the Three Bibles on London Bridge" (*T.C.* III, 674). Copies are in B.M.L. (1268.a.39); B.L.O. (302.g.141); R.L.M. (Bailey coll., 514.K.78); C.L.M. (Harland coll., Mun.D.2.4); U.L.C. (Adams.7.71.1); C.L.E. (Pocknell coll., 507R/653); P.L.L.; N.L.S. (Warden coll., Wn.871); and L.N.Y. (Howard coll., *IDE).

"The obstacles in the way of compiling a reliable and exhaustive Shelton bibliography are probably insuperable", wrote A. T. Wright (*Thomas Shelton, Tachygrapher*, 1896). The bibliography of Shelton's "Tachygraphy" is particularly perplexing, many of the copies now extant being, as Mr Wright pointed out, made-up copies. Few of them contain the portrait of Shelton which was originally prefixed to more than one edition. The foregoing list makes no pretension to completeness, though I have been at pains to make it as accurate as possible.

A Tvtor | to | Tachygraphy, | or, | Short-vvriting, | Wherein the Rules of the said | Art, are severally explained by way | of Questions and Answers, to | the weakest capacities that desire | to learne the Art. | *Whereunto are added;* | Diverse new Rules and Directions | never published till now, for the fur- | ther perfecting of such as have al- | ready Learned. | By Thomas Shelton, | *Author and teacher of the said Art.* | Printed at *London* for *Samuel Cartwright,* | and are to be sold at the hand and | Bible in *Duck-lane.* 1642.   [402ᴵᴵ.]

5¾ × 3½ in., 8vo, pp. (4) + 36 letterpress. With headlines. Title within border of printer's ornaments. Sign. A–C4 in eights. The shorthand characters in the text are printed from woodcuts.

Leaf 1ᵃ Title, 1ᵇ blank, 2ᵃ–2ᵇ To the Reader, 3ᵃ–19ᵃ Text, 19ᵇ–20ᵇ Examples.

There were three variant editions of Shelton's "Tutor" dated 1642, and it is difficult now to determine their order of precedence. Copies of the edition described above are in B.M.L. (C.31.a.49.(2)); P.L.L.; and W.J.C.

Another edition, with a similar title, has the imprint: "*London*, Printed by M. S. and are to be sold at the Authors house in Olde Fish-street, 1642." The printer was Matthew Simmons. This edition consists of pp. (4)+52 letterpress. The address to the reader is dated at the end "From my house in Old Fish-street, May 3. 1642." Copies are in the libraries of the Institute of Shorthand Writers, London, and S.L.D. (C.a.3ª).

A third edition, with a similar title, has the imprint: "London Printed by E. P. and are to bee sold at the Authors house in Old-Fish-street. 1642." The printer was probably Elizabeth Purslow. This edition also consists of pp. (4)+52, the address to the reader being dated 3 May 1642. Copies are in B.M.L. (C.31.a.48); C.L.M. (2.I.1.66); Sion College, London (L.30.4.Sh.4); N.L.S. (Warden coll., Wn.867); L.C.W. (Z56.S545T); L.N.Y. (Beale coll., Reserve), W.J.C. and C.E.B. (Havette coll.).

A reissue of the 1642 edition with the imprint of Samuel Cartwright, but with the date altered to 1643, is in B.M.L. (C.31.a.46.(4)); N.L.S. (Warden coll., Wn.864, incomplete); B.L.M.; and W.J.C.

A reprint of the 1642 edition with the imprint "Printed by M. S.", limited to 100 copies, was issued by Robert McCaskie, bookseller, London, in 1889. Copies are in B.M.L. (12991.c.49); L.N.Y. (Beale coll.); W.J.C., etc.

A "corrected and enlarged" edition, 1645, was included in "A Catalogue of the Library of the late John Byrom", printed in 1848, but is not to be found among Byrom's books in C.L.M. This entry may be due to confusion with the 1645 edition of "Tachygraphy".

Shelton's "Tutor to Tachygraphy" is usually found bound together with "Tachygraphy", the two works having been issued in a single volume.

Tachy-graphia | sive | Exactissima & compendiosis- | sima breviter Scriben- | di methodus. | Primitus composita in Lingua | Anglicana, | Per | *Thomam Shelton* | utilissimæ illius artis Authorem. | Et jam in publicum totius Europae | usum Latinè edocta loqui. | *Tachygraphes liber est parvus, sed fructus in illo | Non parvus; parva hæc Virque Puerque pete!* | *Londini,* | excusum pro *Gulielmo Miller,* ad insigne | Glandis deaurati, in Cæmeterio Paulino, | juxta Ostiolum Boreale, 1671. [402¹.]

5⅝ × 3½ in., 8vo, pp. (6)+17 (numbered 1–14)+(6) letterpress, with 14 plates engraved on one or both sides. With headlines. Sign. A–D4 in fours.

Leaf 1ᵃ blank, 1ᵇ Bust portrait of Shelton with engraved title, 2ᵃ Letterpress title-page, 2ᵇ blank, 3ᵃ–3ᵇ Prefatio Candido Lectori, 4ᵃ Animadversio, 4ᵇ Artis Tachygraphicæ Alphabetum, 5ᵃ–5ᵇ Text, 6ᵃ Duplices Consonantes, 6ᵇ Vocalium locus, 7ᵃ–7ᵇ Text, 8ᵃ Examples, 8ᵇ blank, 9ᵃ–9ᵇ Text, 10ᵃ Examples, 10ᵇ blank, 11ᵃ Examples, 11ᵇ blank, 12ᵃ Text, 12ᵇ–13ᵃ blank, 13ᵇ–14ᵃ Prepositiones et Terminationes, 14ᵇ blank, 15ᵃ–15ᵇ Text, 16ᵃ blank, 16ᵇ–17ᵇ Text, 18ᵃ Exempla verborum prioribus signis conscriptorum, 18ᵇ blank, 19ᵃ Exempla, 19ᵇ blank, 20ᵃ–21ᵃ Text, 21ᵇ Verborum primum Exemplum secundum regulam, 22ᵃ blank, 22ᵇ Verborum secundum exemplum, 23ᵃ Verborum tertium exemplum, 23ᵇ–24ᵃ blank, 24ᵇ Verborum quartum exemplum, 25ᵃ Quintum Verborum Exemplum, 25ᵇ–26ᵃ blank, 26ᵇ Sextum Verborum Exemplum, 27ᵃ Verborum Septimum Exemplum, 27ᵇ blank, 28ᵃ De rebus in urbe & Regione (Latin phrases in shorthand and longhand), 28ᵇ blank, 29ᵃ De rebus (contd.), 29ᵇ blank, 30ᵃ De rebus (contd.), 30ᵇ blank.

This appears to have been the second edition of the Latin version of Shelton's "Tachygraphy". It was announced in the Term Catalogue, Easter 1671, as "Printed for W. Miller at the Acorn in St. Paul's Churchyard. In Octavo. Price, stich't, 1s." (*T.C.* 1, 74). Copies of this edition are in B.M.L. (1043.a.54); B.L.O. (8° Q.8.Th.); U.L.C. (Bb12.38⁶(F), lacking engraved title and portrait); R.L.M. (Bailey coll., 514.K.72).

The first edition, with the same title, carries the imprint: "*Londini,* Excudebat *Tho. Creake,* 1660." Prefixed is the same engraved title-page, with portrait, as in the 1671 edition. Copies are in C.L.E. (Pocknell coll., 508R/653);

B.N.P. (V.25037, lacking engraved title and portrait); Sächsische Landesbibliothek, Dresden (Graphica 529); and L.N.Y. (Howard coll., Reserve).

Zeiglographia. | or | *A New art of Short-writing* | *never before published.* | *More easie, exact, short, and* | *speedie then any heretofore.* | *Invented & composed* | *By* | *Thomas Shelton* | *Author and teacher of ỹ* | *said art* | *Allowed by Authoritie* | London | Printed *for Dor* | *Newman at the* | *Kings Armes in ỹ* | *Poultry & Thomas* | *Sawbridge in* | *Little* | *Brittaine.* | 1685. [860¹¹.]

6½ × 3½ in., 8vo, pp. (4) + 56 letterpress, except the title-page and last page which are engraved. With headlines. Sign. (A–A2), B–E4 in eights. The running title is "A New Art of Short-Writing". Each page of letterpress is within a border of printer's ornaments.

Leaf 1ᵃ Title, 1ᵇ blank, 2ᵃ–2ᵇ "To the Reader", 3ᵃ–22ᵃ Text, 22ᵇ–27ᵃ A table of the usual English words, 27ᵇ–30ᵃ Text, 30ᵇ Arms and crest above the Lord's Prayer, Creed and Ten Commandments in shorthand.

This is a late edition of "Zeiglographia". It was announced in the Term Catalogue, Hilary 1685, as "sold by D. Newman at the King's Arms in the Poultrey, and T. Sawbridge at the Three Flower de Luces in Little Britain" (*T.C.* II, 119). Copies are in B.M.L. (51.a.19), R.L.M. (Bailey coll., 514.K.75), J.R.G. and W.J.C. (W. F. Mavor's copy).

The first edition was entered on the Stationers' Register to "Master Symmons" [i.e. Matthew Simmons] on 7 June 1649, "provided the author of this copie be not Mʳ Shelton" (Roxb. *Transcript*, I, 319). The clerk who made the entries in the Register at this time was a writer of shorthand, possibly knew Shelton and Samuel Cartwright, and had his doubts about Simmons's right to enter the work. On the following 25 January 1649/50, however, "Tachigraphy, or the art of short writing with the Tutor thereunto & Zeiglography, or, a new art of short writing, all of them composed by Thomas Shelton & with his full consent", were entered to Cartwright and Simmons "by vertue of a note under their hands & seales" (Roxb.

39

Transcript, I, 336). By an assignment of the same date Cartwright transferred his half-interest in the three works to Simmons. The first edition has the same title as that of 1685, but the imprint reads: "London *Printed by M. S. and are sold at the Authors house in the Poultrie nere ỹ Church And at ỹ Blew Anchor in Cornhill.* 1650". The title-page is engraved within a wreath of laurels, surmounted by two crossed quill pens fastened by a ribbon. In the bottom left-hand corner is "J: G: [i.e. J. Glover] sculp:", and the same initials are at the foot of the last (engraved) page. This edition contains a dedicatory epistle "To the supream authority of England" which is not found in those issued subsequent to the Restoration. The address "To the Reader" is dated "From my House in the Poultry, near the Church. *Septemb.* 10. 1649. Thomas Shelton." A copy is in W.J.C.

Another edition dated 1650 has a similar title-page with the imprint: "London *Printed by M. S. and are sold at the Authors house in the Poultrie nere ỹ Church* 1650". Copies are in N.L.S. (Warden coll., Wn.868); B.L.O. (25788.f.398); L.N.Y. (Beale coll., *IDS p.v.75, no. 4); U.L.Y. (Healey coll., F25.362); and W.J.C.

Another edition has a similar title-page with the imprint: "London Printed *by M. S. and are sold at the Authors house in Bores-head Court by Cripple-Gate* 1654". The title-page has been re-engraved and the engraver's initials are almost effaced. The text of the work has been reset, the date at the end of the address to the reader being omitted. Copies of this edition are in C.L.W. (Walford coll.); J.R.G. (Todd coll., wanting title-page); and W.J.C. (wanting last leaf). A copy was in the Huth library.

Matthew Simmons, the printer, died 19 May 1654. His widow seems to have continued his business and five years afterwards acquired Samuel Cartwright's interest. On 19 April 1659 she was entered on the Stationers' Register, "by vertue of an assignment under the hand & seale of Samuell Cartwright, all his estate, right, & title (being one full moyetie or half part thereof) in the bookes or copies following, vizt, Tachigraphy, or the art of short writing with the tutor thereunto, and Zeiglography, or a new art of short writing, all of them written by Thomas Shelton. To wch assignm^t ye hand of Master Pulleyn ward. is subscribed" (Roxb. *Transcript*, II, 222).

40

A reissue of the 1654 edition with the same title-page except for the alteration of the date to 1659 was published in the latter year. Copies are in B.M.L. (1042.c.31); C.L.M. (Harland coll., Mun.D.1.85); N.L.S. (Warden coll., Wn.869); B.N.P. (V. Réserve 2459); L.N.Y. (Howard coll., Reserve); and the libraries of Sir F. Newdegate, Nuneaton, and W.J.C.

A variant edition dated 1659, with the same title-page but the letterpress reset, is in W.J.C.

Another edition has a similar title-page with the imprint: "London *Printed by S. S.* [i.e. Samuel Simmons] *Next door to the Golden Lion in Aldersgate Streete* 1672". This edition was announced in the Term Catalogue, Hilary 1672, as "printed for M. Simmons, and are to be sold by the several Booksellers of London. 1s." (*T.C.* I, 99). Copies are in B.M.L. (787.a.74.(2)); B.L.O. (302.g.144); N.L.S. (Warden coll., Wn.850); C.L.W. (Walford coll.); L.N.Y. (Beale coll., Reserve); J.R.G. (Todd coll.); and W.J.C.

A reprint is announced in the Term Catalogue, Trinity 1687, as "printed for D. Newman at King's Arms in the Poultrey" (*T.C.* II, 203). No copy with this date has been located.

Another reprint was announced in the Term Catalogue, Easter 1689, as "sold by T. Speed at the Crown in the Poultrey" (*T.C.* II, 263). No copy with such an imprint or date is recorded.

Another reprint was announced in the Term Catalogue, Michaelmas 1690, as "printed for T. Speed at the Three Crowns in Cornhill" (*T.C.* II, 341). No copy is recorded.

Another reprint was announced in the Term Catalogue, Hilary 1693, as "printed for Tho. Speed at the Three Crowns in Cornhill" (*T.C.* II, 444). No copy is recorded.

An undated edition has a similar title-page to that of 1685 with the imprint: "London *Printed for ỹ Booksellers. Price 1ˢ.*" This edition was announced in the Term Catalogue, Michaelmas 1706, as "printed for the Booksellers of London and Westminster" (*T.C.* III, 528). Copies are in B.M.L. (Fraser coll., 1042.b.78); R.L.M. (Bailey coll., 514.K.79); N.L.S. (Warden coll., Wn.872); and W.J.C. (wanting title-page and last leaf).

41

The last recorded edition of "Zeiglographia" has a similar title-page with the imprint: "London Printed for *E. Tracy* at 3 Bibles on London Bridge". Eben (or Ebenezer) Tracy was publishing at this address from 1696 to 1712, and the date is approximately fixed by the Term Catalogue, Easter 1711, which announces an edition as "printed for E. Tracy at the Three Bibles on London Bridge" (*T.C.* III, 674). Copies are in B.M.L. (12991.b.31) and L.N.Y. (Beale coll., Reserve).

The only other known shorthand work by Shelton is the Book of Psalms engraved throughout in his system by Thomas Cross, and published in a small volume measuring $2\frac{1}{2} \times 1\frac{1}{2}$ in. with a frontispiece portrait of Shelton. Both in size and presentation it bears a striking resemblance to the volume containing the Psalms engraved by Cross in Rich's shorthand (see p. 60), which according to Rich's own statement "has bene promised by others but never was performed by any". At least two editions of Shelton's Psalms were printed. Neither of them is dated, but both were published posthumously and were doubtless booksellers' ventures. The earlier edition was probably printed before 1679; its title-page reads: "The Whole Book of Psalms *in Meeter According to that most exact & Compendious method of* Short Writing *Composed by* Thomas Shelton (*Being his former hand*) *aproued by both Vniversities & learnt by many thousands. Sold by* Iohn Clarke *at Mercers Chappell in cheap-side T: Cross sculpsit.*" Two copies of this edition are in L.N.Y. (Rockwell and Beale collections, *KVM, the latter incomplete).

Another edition has a similar title-page with the imprint: "*Sold by Tho: Cockerill at the three Leggs and Bible in the Poultrey T: Cross Sculpsit*". It was probably not published before 1679. Copies are in B.M.L. (C.17.a.27, wanting publisher's address "To the Reader"); B.L.O. (Arch.Bodl. A.III.10); British & Foreign Bible Society, London (HC.553.b); W.J.C.

Thomas Shelton contrived two distinct shorthand systems, which have sometimes been confused. The earlier of them, expounded first in his "Short Writing" (1626) and afterwards in "Tachygraphy" (1635), was the one which Pepys wrote, and it attained wide popularity. The alphabet was mainly that of Edmond Willis, though two of John Willis's compound signs (those for *a* and *c*) were reinstated and a new character for *e* was adopted from the secretary hand. Shelton's method of vowel representation differed in no essential respect from that of Edmond Willis, but he simplified the writing of diphthongs by making no attempt to distinguish the exact vowel sounds of which they were composed and contenting himself with indicating the accented vowel. An initial vowel could be omitted "when the sound of it is drowned in the sound of the next letter following". Thus, when initial *e* was followed by *m, n, s* or *x*, only the consonant sign was written, the preceding vowel being that indicated by the pronunciation of the consonant, as in *empty, end, escape, extent* (written *mpty, nd, scape, xtent*). He deprecated the use of arbitrary signs to represent sentences and judiciously observed: "To make many marks for whole sentences is needlesse; because by the rules of this Art, any thing may be written word for word, as fast as it shall be treatably spoken. And it is indeed impossible to use them exactly, because sometimes the speaker varying a word or two in the sentence, the mark is either of no use, or else the sentence must be rendered in other words than it was spoken, which is a wrong to the speaker. Therefore I have only abbreviated a few, which commonly are spoken in the very words as I have set them down."

Shelton's second system, "Zeiglographia", although the outcome of more than thirty years' study and practice and frequently reprinted, did not meet with the same success as the earlier one. The alphabet was entirely recast, the only characters of "Tachygraphy" retained being those for *e, r, u* and *z*. The author's aim was "so to frame the letters, to fit with each other, that none could be composed to more advantage for speed"; but he still had recourse to many compound signs which militated against rapid writing. The signs for prefixes and suffixes, or "prepositions" and "terminations" as he called them, were derived from the alphabet in every case, a great improvement on the arbitrary symbols of his first system, which bore little or no relation to the alphabetical characters.

THOMAS SHELTON (1601–1650?) sprang from an old Norfolk family. The year of his birth is derived from portraits which give his age as 46 in 1647 and 49 in 1650, but nothing is known of his parentage and early years. The arms of the Shelton and Hussey families appear to be counterchanged in the

43

armorial bearings which adorn most of his books. Shelton, who may have begun his career as a writing master, had taken up the study of shorthand before he was 19, and his first published work, "Short Writing", was printed in London in 1626. Four years later, when a second edition appeared, he was living in Cheapside, "over against Bowe Church", within the parish of All Hallows, Honey Lane. Two sons and two daughters were born during his residence there, their baptisms being recorded in the parish register—Thomas, on 11 January 1631; Elizabeth, on 24 January 1632; Sarah, on 4 May 1633; and Christopher, on 7 August 1635. Elizabeth died in infancy and was buried in the cloister of All Hallows on 25 January 1633.

Whilst living in Cheapside Shelton prepared a new manual of his art to which he gave the title of "Tachygraphy", the first edition being printed at the Cambridge University Press in 1635. It was described on the title-page as "approoued by both Vnyuersities", but this may mean no more than that the Vice-Chancellor's licence had been obtained for it to be printed within the limits of the universities. Evidence of the author's allegiance to the Puritan party is found in the fact that both "Short Writing" and "Tachygraphy" were dedicated to his "very worthy friend Mr. Richard Knightly, Esquire", who was also the friend of Pym and Hampden. The religious fervour exhibited in some passages of his shorthand treatises inspired his next literary production, "A Centvrie of Similies", printed in 1640. It consists of similes suggested by various biblical texts, of which he offered "a few for a tast" before venturing to publish the "far greater number" originally intended. In April 1640 Thomas Shelton, "of the parish of St. Anne, Blackfriars, London, Chyrographer", was summoned to appear before the Court of High Commission on a charge which is not specified, though its nature may be surmised from the fact that a month later John Dawson and Ralph Mabb, of whom the former had sponsored the "Century of Similies", were cited with him as co-defendants. The proceedings resulted in a commission being decreed on 26 November, but the delinquents were probably saved from any serious consequences by the abolition of the Court of High Commission in 1641.

In 1641 Shelton is found living in Old Fish Street near Bread Street Hill, whence he issued in the spring of 1642 "A Tutor to Tachygraphy" for the benefit of his pupils. His success as a teacher must have been considerable, and his system was widely practised. Simon West, a bookseller at the Blackamoor's

Head in Great Wood Street, near Cheapside, in his "Arts Improuement or Short and Swift Writing" (1647), claimed to have "writ after one of the best approved Professours of this Art, these seven years", the initials T. S. in the margin clearly indicating the identity of the professor. S. Shelton, the author of "Brachygraphy" (1672), declared that he had received his first instructions in the art more than 30 years previously from his old friend and namesake, Mr Shelton.

By 1645 Shelton had removed to a house in the Poultry "near the church", as the title-page of an edition of "Tachygraphy" printed in that year shows. On 10 September 1649 he wrote there the preface to his last shorthand work, "Zeiglographia", embodying an entirely new system which was an "abstract of more than thirty years' study and practice" in the art, and dedicated it "To the Supream Authority of England". The Commonwealth had been established only eight months previously. "It was my purpose that this Child should not have been borne till the Parent had been dead", he tells his readers, and there is reason to believe that he did not long survive its publication. Matthew Simmons, the printer of "Zeiglographia", was also the printer of "Mercurius Politicus", and in No. 18 of that news sheet, dated 3–10 October 1650, he announced that an edition of Shelton's "Zeiglographica", "being his last 30. years study", was to be sold by M. Simmons in Aldersgate Street, next door to the Golden Lion. It is true that on the engraved title-page of the 1654 edition the address in the Poultry was replaced by "the Author's house in Bore's Head Court by Cripplegate", but as the old address is retained in the text the inference seems to be that Shelton was then in his grave. In 1650 appeared "Divine Drops distilled from the Fountain of Holy Scriptures", a series of twenty-three "exercises before sermons" by the Puritan preacher Walter Cradock, with an address to the reader signed Thomas Shelton. From this address it appears that the exercises were printed from Shelton's shorthand notes, as were many sermons of Richard Sibbs, John Preston, Martin Day, Henry Ramsden, Josiah Shute and other Puritan divines.

Shelton's shorthand books were frequently reprinted, a Latin version of "Tachygraphia" appearing in 1660, and his fame spread to the Continent. An allusion to Thomas Shelton's art in Randolph's "Hey for Honesty" (1651) shows that at that date Shelton and shorthand were practically synonymous terms. As late as 1736 Philip Gibbs, in his "Historical Account of Compendious and Swift Writing", writing of Shelton and Metcalfe, observed that "their Books may easily be come at, and, by many, their Methods are very well known, and still continue to be practised".

(A. T. Wright's *Thomas Shelton, Tachygrapher* (1896), and *Addenda* (1897); *Notes and Queries,* CLXV, 326 (11 Nov. 1933); *Phonetic Journal,* XLV, 105–7 (27 Feb. 1886); LXII, 102, 103, 123 (7 and 14 Feb. 1903); Sir Ambrose Heal's *The English Writing-Masters and their Copy-Books, 1570–1800,* 1931, p. 96.)

The | Art | of | Brachygraphy | or | *Short-writing,* | By Characters faire, short, | swift, easie and legible. | *Plainly taught by this Booke.* | Composed by Henry Dix. | The third Edition. | *London:* | Printed for *T. B.* and are to be sold by | the Author at the signe of the guilded | Anchor in Pater noster row, neere | Cheapside. 1641.

[402⁵.]

5⅝ × 3⅜ in., 16mo, pp. (42) letterpress, including letterpress title as above within woodcut "lace" border, with 1 engraved plate. No numbers to pages. Shorthand characters in MS. and engraved. Sign. A–A2, B–B8, C–C8, 1 leaf headed "The first Table" (verso blank), and 2 leaves headed "The second table". The running title is "The Art of Brachygraphy". The letterpress title-page is preceded by an engraved title by John Droeshout (Johnson, No. 8) within an architectural framework enclosing also the Ten Commandments, the Lord's Prayer and the Creed in shorthand characters. The engraved title reads:

The | Art | of | Brachygraphy | or | shorth writing | by | Characters faire | *Short Speedy* | Easie and | Legible | *Plainly Taught* | By this *Booke* | *Composed by* | Henry Dix | London | *Printed for the* | *Author and are* | *to be sold by him* | *at the Golden An* | *chor in Pater noster* | *Row neere cheape* | *side where Hee* | *Teacheth this Art* | *Io: Droeshout sculp.*

Leaf 1ᵃ Title (engraved), 1ᵇ blank, 2ᵃ Title (letterpress), 2ᵇ blank, 3ᵃ–3ᵇ "To the Reader" in verse, 4ᵃ–4ᵇ "The Art of Brachygraphy, or Short-Writing",

5^a "The Table (or grounds) of Spelling Charactery" (engraved), 5^b blank, 6^a–13^b The Art of Brachygraphy, 14^a The first Table, 14^b blank, 15^a–18^b The Art of Brachygraphy, 19^a–20^b The second Table, 21^a–23^b The Art of Brachygraphy, Finis, A Post-script to the Reader.

The Pepysian copy lacks the engraved title-page. Of the two copies in B.M.L. only one (C.31.a.46.(5)), formerly the property of James Henry Lewis, the shorthand historian, is complete. The other (1043.b.51) lacks the two leaves headed "The second Table". No other copy of this edition has been located.

The first edition of Dix's "Art of Brachygraphy" was entered on the Stationers' Register to Thomas Brudnell on 10 June 1633 (Arber's *Transcript*, IV, 297). Its title was: "A | Nevv Art Of | Brachygraphy; | *or,* | Short-vvriting | By Characters. | More faire, short, swift, lineall, | and Legible, than any forme of | Short-writing, formerly pub- | *lished by any.* | Plainly taught, by such facile Rules, that | (even) meane capacities may with much | speed attaine to the Knowledge of | *this Art, by this Booke, with-* | out any other Teacher. | Composed by *Henry Dix.* | [Line ornament] | Printed at *London* for the Author, and are to | be sold at his Shop at the Golden Anchor | in *Paternoster*-Row, neere *Cheap-* | *side,* 1633." Two copies only are known: one in C.L.W. (Walford coll.), the other in the N.L.S. (Warden coll., Wn.827, with MS. additions and corrections by the author).

No copy of the second edition of the book has been traced.

Dix's shorthand was based on that of John Willis (see p. 19), which he followed fairly closely in its main lines, though a few of his alphabetical characters are different. He retained two sizes of characters, but reduced the vowel places to three, *a, e, o,* which he called "constant vowels", being indicated by juxtaposition, *i, u* by disjunction. By indicating the vowels only on the right side of the consonantal signs, he avoided the retrograde pen movements necessitated by the systems of most of his predecessors. He also introduced some improvements in the direction of lineality and provided special signs for a number of double consonants.

47

HENRY DIX (fl. 1633–1641) had a shop in Paternoster Row, near Cheapside, at the sign of the Golden Anchor, in 1633, and he was teaching shorthand there in 1641. He is probably identical with the Henry Dicks who appears in a return of householders in the parish of St Michael Le Quern made in 1638 (*The Inhabitants of the City of London in 1638*, ed. T. C. Dale, 1931, p. 152). The church of St Michael Le Quern stood at the angle of Paternoster Row and St Paul's Churchyard, but was burned down in the Great Fire when the earlier register was destroyed and the parish was united with that of St Vedast, Foster Lane. The register of the latter church records the burial of Ann Dicks on 10 September 1652.

Dix appears to have been a man of some literary talent, the verses printed in the third edition of his manual being considerably above the standard of those usually found in works of that period. One of his predecessors at the Golden Anchor, John Harrison the younger, was a bookseller and issued an edition of Spenser's minor poems from that address in 1617. Josias Harrison, son of John, was a bookseller at the Golden Anchor from 1615 to 1619 (McKerrow, 1557–1640, p. 127). A Henry Dicks was buried at All Hallows, London Wall, on 23 November 1665, but no evidence has been found to connect him with the author of "The Art of Brachygraphy".

Short-Writing, | *The most easie, Exact, Lineal, and Spee-* | *dy Method that hath ever been Ob-* | *tained, or Taught.* | Composed by | Theophilus Metcalfe, | Author and Professor of the said | Art. | The Last Edition. | *With a New Table for shortning of Words.* | Which Book is able to make the Pra- | ctitioner perfect without a Teacher. | As many Hundreds in this City, and | elsewhere, that are able to write Sermons | word for word, can from their own Expe- | rience Testifie. | A young man, that lately lived in | *Cornhil*, Learned so well by this Book, | that he wrote out all the Bible in this | Character. | *London*, Printed for, and are to be sold | by *J. Hancock* near the *Royal Exchange* in | *Cornhil*. 1690.   [860², 860⁶.]

6½ × 3½ in., pp. 16 letterpress and 22 engraved leaves printed on one side (including frontispiece portrait of Metcalfe and engraved title). The shorthand characters in the text are engraved on wood. The running title is

"The Art of Short-writing". Sign. A–A8. The letterpress title is within a border of printer's rules and is preceded by an engraved title within an architectural framework enclosing also the Ten Commandments and the Lord's Prayer in shorthand characters. The engraved title reads as follows:

Short | Writing the most Easie, | Exact lineall and speedy | Method that hath ever yet | been obtained or taught. | Composed by | Theophilus Metcalfe | Author and professor | of the said Art | [Here follow the Commandments and the Lord's Prayer in shorthand characters] | The 19th | Edition much in- | larged by the Author | which is able to make the | practicioner perfect with- | out any other Teacher | London printed for | Io: Hancock & are to be | sold at his shop at the | entrance into pops | head Alle out of | Cornhill | Cross sculp. |

Leaf 1^a blank, 1^b Portrait of Metcalfe with 8 lines of verse below, 2^a Engraved title, 2^b blank, 3^a Letterpress title, 3^b blank, 4^a–4^b To the Reader and The Stationer to the Reader, 5^a–5^b Text, 6^a blank, 6^b Alphabet and double consonants, 7^a–8^b Text, 9^a blank, 9^b Examples, 10^a blank, 10^b Third and fourth rules, 11^a Fifth rule, 11^b–12^a blank, 12^b Sixth to tenth rules, 13^a Eleventh to fourteenth rules, 13^b blank, 14^a Prepositions and terminations, 14^b blank, 15^a–17^b Text, 18^a blank, 18^b–19^a Examples of words, 19^b–20^a blank, 21^b Examples illustrating Chapters 8 and 9, 22^a Abbreviations illustrating Chapter 10, 22^b–23^a blank, 23^b Hard names in Scripture, 24^a Names of the Bookes of the Old and New Testament, 24^b blank, 25^a Of the use of points and Of the table of words, 25^b–26^a blank, 26^b–27^a The table, 27^b–28^a blank, 28^b–29^a The table, 29^b–30^a blank, 30^b Of joyning words and Of the abbreviation of sentences, 31^a Abbreviations of sentences, 31^b blank.

This is a late issue of Metcalfe's "Short-Writing", probably the one announced in the Term Catalogue, Michaelmas 1690 (*T.C.* II, 341). Two copies are bound up in the same volume in the Pepysian Library, and at the foot of one of these Pepys has written: "N.B. That a useless Double hereof is by mistake to be found Pag. 297." Other copies are in B.G.P. (Guénin coll., Δ 68172, wanting portrait) and W.J.C. (with the engraved title-page of the 35th ed., 1698, prefixed).

No copy of the first edition of Metcalfe's shorthand is known to be extant. It was entered on the Stationers' Register to William Jones on 18 April 1633 as "a booke called The Art of Stenography, by Theodore Medcalfe", with an appended note intimating that the widow of William Jones had later "surrendred vp to the Author to be by him disposed of" the copyright of the book (Arber's *Transcript*, IV, 295). No copy of any edition between the first and the sixth has been traced.

An apparently unique copy of the first issue of the 6th edition, 1645, is in B.M.L. (Lewis coll., C.31.a.46.(1)). It has an engraved title-page (Johnson, No. 2) reading as follows: "*Short Writing the most Easie Exact lineall and speedy Method that hath ever yet been obtained or taught by any in this Kingdome. Composed by Theophilus Metcalfe Author and professor of the said Art.... The sixt Edition much inlarged by the Author which is able to make the practicioner perfect without any other Teachor London printed for the Author sould at his house in Sᵗ Katherins Court neare the Tower, & at Mʳ Simpsons house in Oxford Court right agˢᵗ London stone. Cross sculp 1645.*"

A second issue of the 6th edition has the same engraved title-page prefixed, but the imprint has been altered to read: "*London: printed by Io: Hancock & are to be sold at his shop at the entrance into pop's Head alle out of Cornhill 1646.*" This edition was entered on the Stationers' Register to John Hancock on 10 April 1646 "by vertue of a bill of sale under yᵉ hand & seale of Mʳˢ Medcalfe widd" (Roxb. *Transcript*, I, 224). Copies are in B.M.L. (12991.b.3); B.N.P. (V.11193 bis); and W.J.C. The engraved portrait of Metcalfe by Thomas Cross was probably done for this edition.

A copy of the seventh edition, with the date 1649 on the engraved title-page and a letterpress title dated 1650, is in B.M.L. (7942.a.19).

The eighth edition has an engraved title-page without date and a letterpress title dated 1652. Copies are in B.M.L. (1042.c.30); C.L.W. (Walford coll., lacking plate 20); and L.N.Y. (Howard coll., Reserve).

A copy of the ninth edition, with the engraved title-page of the eighth edition and letterpress title-page dated 1657, is in W.J.C. It lacks plates 37, 38 and 39. The "table of examples for shortning of words" appeared first in this edition.

An edition called "the last edition", dated 1660 on the letterpress title-page, is in F.L.W. The British Museum has an imperfect copy (1043.b.53), lacking the portrait, engraved title-page and leaves 38 and 39.

Another edition, called the 9th edition on the engraved title-page, is also called "the last edition" on the letterpress title-page, which bears the following imprint: "*London* Printed, and are to be sold by *John Hancock* at his shop in *Bishopsgate* street over against Gresham Colledge, next to the *White Lyon*, at great St. Hellens Gate, 1668." Copies are in L.C.W. (Z56.M58 S9) and S.L.D. (C.a.6).

Another edition, with an engraved title-page bearing "9th edition", is called "the last edition" on the letterpress title-page, which has the following imprint: "*London*, Printed for, and are to be sold by *John Hancock* at the first Shop in *Popes-Head-Alley* in *Cornhil*, at the sign of the three Bibles, or at his Shop in *Bishops-Gate-Street*, near great St. *Hellens, over against Gresham Colledg.* 1669." Copies are in B.M.L. (787.b.82); C.L.M. (Harland coll., Mun.D2.6); N.L.S. (Warden coll., Wn.846, wanting engraved title); and the library of Sir F. Newdegate, Nuneaton.

An edition was announced in the Term Catalogue, Michaelmas 1674, under "Books Reprinted" (*T.C.* 1, 191). Some copies with the engraved title-page of the "9th edition" have a letterpress title-page dated 1674, the imprint reading: "*London*, Printed for, and are to be sold by *John Hancock* at the first Shop in *Popes-Head-Alley* in *Cornhil*, at the sign of the three Bibles, 1674." A copy is in W.J.C. (W. F. Mavor's copy).

Copies with the same letterpress title-page and date but with "10th edition" on the engraved title-page are in P.L.L. L.C.W. (Z56.M58 S10); L.N.Y. (Howard coll., Reserve) and the Library of the American Antiquarian Society, Worcester, Mass. (Cummings coll.).

An edition was announced in the Term Catalogue, Hilary 1677, under "Reprinted" (*T.C.* 1, 270). No copy with this date has been located.

Another "last edition", with the engraved title-page of the "19th edition", has the following imprint on the letterpress title-page: "*London*, Printed for, and are sold by *John Hancock* at the first Shop in *Popes-Head-Alley* in *Cornhil*, at the sign of the three Bibles, 1679." Copies are in B.M.L. (1042.b.57); N.L.S. (Warden coll., Wn.849); C.L.W.; and W.J.C. The copies in U.L.C. (L.32.56²) and L.N.Y. (Rockwell coll., *IDE) lack the engraved title-page.

A copy described as the tenth edition, 1681, on the letterpress title-page is in C.L.W. (Walford coll.), with engraved title-page and portrait.

Another "last edition" has the following imprint on the letterpress title-page: "*London*, Printed for *John Hancock* near the Royal-Exchange in *Cornhil*. 1698." The copy in B.M.L. (G.16758.(2)) has an engraved title-page called "35th Edition" with the same date. The copy in W.J.C. lacks the engraved title-page and the portrait. Another copy is in the Harvard University Library.

Another "last edition" has the following imprint on the letterpress title-page: "*London:* Printed for *John Hancock*, and to be Sold by *M. Hotham*, at the *Black-Boy* on *London-Bridge*, 1706." An engraved title-page, with the same date but "55th edition", is prefixed. This edition was announced in the Term Catalogue, Hilary 1706 (*T.C.* III, 499). Copies are in B.M.L. (7942.aa.39); B.L.O. (302.g.152.(9)); R.L.M. (Bailey coll., 514.H.82); C.L.M. (2 copies, Mun.D2.7 & 8); N.L.S. (Warden coll., Wn.847); L.N.Y. (Beale coll., *IDE p.v.13, no. 5); J.R.G.; and W.J.C.

A later issue was announced in the Term Catalogue, Michaelmas 1707 (*T.C.* III, 577). No copy of this issue has been identified.

The last known edition of Metcalfe's "Short-Writing" is called the 55th edition on both letterpress and engraved title-pages. The imprint on the former is "*London:* Printed for *Edmund Parker*, at the *Bible* and *Crown* in *Lombard-Street.* 1721.", and on the latter "*London Sold by* Edmund Parker *In Lombard-Street.*" Copies are in B.M.L. (Fraser coll., 1042.b.72, date erased from title-page); I.S.W.; C.L.E. (Pocknell coll.); N.L.S. (Warden coll., Wn.848); and W.J.C.

In 1649 was published another work by Metcalfe, entitled "A Schoolmaster to Radio-Stenography, Explaining All the Rules of the said Art, by way of Dialogue betwixt Master and Scholler. Fitted to the weakest capacities that are desirous to learne this Art. Composed by Theophilus Metcalfe, Author and Professor of the said Art. *London*, Printed, and are to be sold by *John*

Hancock at the first shop in *Popes-head Alley*, next to Corn-hill. 1649."
A copy is in B.M.L. (7942.a.20), to which Metcalfe's portrait and the
engraved title-page of the 9th edition of his "Short-Writing" are prefixed.
The address to the reader refers to the 7th edition of "Short-Writing", to
which the "Schoolmaster" was intended to serve as a companion on the
lines of John Willis's "School-Master to the Art of Stenography" (see p. 17)
and Thomas Shelton's "Tutor to Tachygraphy" (see p. 36). Another
copy, wanting portrait and title-page, is in C.L.W. (Fraser and Walford coll.).

A later edition of Metcalfe's "Schoolmaster" was published in 1668 with
the imprint: "*London*, Printed, and are to be sold, by *John Hancock*, at his
shop in *Bishopsgate*-street over against *Gresham* Colledge, next to the *White
Lion*, at great St. *Hellens* Gate, 1668." Copies are in the C.L.M. (Harland
coll., 4B.1.12) and N.L.S. (Warden coll., Wn.849(2)).

Metcalfe was indebted to Shelton's "Tachygraphy" for most of his rules as
well as for ten of his alphabetic characters, but he provided alternative signs
for *h*, *p* and *s*. He also adopted Shelton's method of vowel indication, initial
vowels being expressed by their alphabetic sign, medial vowels by the position
of the following consonant, and final vowels by a dot in the vowel's place.
The plural was shown by a dot on the left. The prefixes and suffixes had to
be learned by heart, having "but small dependance on the letters of the
alphabet". Metcalfe exhorts the learner "not to feare your owne imbecillity,
or weaknesse of your capacitie for the attaining of mature perfection in this
art, by this Booke alone", claiming that "many hundred men and women,
in this City of London", had learned from his book without the aid of a
teacher. Isaac Watts, the hymn-writer, used Metcalfe's shorthand regularly
between 1719 and 1741, and recommended its use in his "Improvement of
the Mind". James Weston, the author of "Stenography Compleated",
1727, adopted Metcalfe's alphabet in its entirety, declaring it to be "the best
that is, or can be, contrived".

THEOPHILUS METCALFE (1610–1646?) was the tenth of eleven
children born to Matthew and Maria Metcalfe of Richmond, Yorkshire, in
which parish he was baptised on 3 June 1610. The Metcalfes of Richmond
traced their descent from James Metcalfe of Beare Park, who was with Henry V

at Agincourt. Theophilus must have married early and appears to have found his way to London by 1633, when his shorthand manual was entered in the Stationers' Register. His three sons Matthew, John and Moses were baptised in the church of St Katherine's by the Tower in 1635, 1638 and 1640 respectively, and the register gives his wife's Christian name as Ann. The title-page of his "Short Writing" of 1645 shows that he then occupied a house in St Katherine's Court, near the Tower, where the book was to be had. This treatise he dedicated to his uncle, Benjamin Taylor, whose "many favours" he acknowledges, and the verses "In Laudem Authoris" prefixed to his "Schoolmaster" and signed "T. T." are doubtless by another uncle, Theophilus Taylor, who was pastor of St Lawrence Church, Reading, from 1618 to 1640. Metcalfe's death must have taken place before 10 April 1646, on which date his widow assigned her rights in his shorthand work to John Hancock (Arber's *Transcript*, I, 224).

In "The Life and Correspondence of Charles, Lord Metcalfe", 1854, Mr J. W. Kaye wrote that "in the reign of Charles the Second [*sic*] Theophilus Metcalfe...was the first to reduce shorthand writing to a system, and to publish an account of it. He went to London, was rewarded for his invention, and in remembrance of it was especially permitted to add a hand and pen to the heraldic adornments of his family escutcheon. He, or his son, afterwards settled in Ireland, and from him the subject of this memoir was lineally descended." The claim that Metcalfe "was the first to reduce shorthand writing to a system" will not bear investigation, and there is no evidence in support of the assertion that the charge of a hand and pen which forms part of the Metcalfe family crest was granted to the stenographer, although it has been repeated by Mr Alexander Paterson (*Phonetic Journal*, LVI, 221, 3 April 1897; LXV, 316, 21 April 1906), quoting from Debrett's "Baronetage", and by Mr Edward Thompson in his recent biography of Lord Metcalfe. From the records in the College of Arms it appears that the crest—a talbot sejant, sable, the dexter paw supporting an escutcheon or—was granted to Matthew Metcalfe, son of Lucas Metcalfe, of Bedale, in 1581; while the charge—a hand, issuant from clouds on the sinister, and holding a pen—was not issued until 1802, when it was granted to Thomas Theophilus Metcalfe, first baronet.

From another source we learn that the stenographer was a grandson of Thomas Metcalfe, of Askrigge (Rev. William Bentham's *Baronetage of*

England, vol. v, Supplementary, 1805, p. 505), that he was heir to a small estate in Yorkshire and was first cousin to Captain Scrope Metcalfe, who commanded the troops raised by the Governor of Oxford and who, dying of the wounds he received at Thame, was buried in St Peter's Church. According to this authority, Theophilus died in London, leaving two daughters and three sons: 1, William, settled in Norfolk as a farmer; 2, Theophilus, bred to the law; 3, John, went abroad to seek his fortune. "Theophilus, the lawyer, having made himself useful to Dykevelt, the Dutch ambassador, was patronised by King William, and went to Ireland in 1690, where he married Peggy Ormsby, by whom he had three sons, William, Theophilus and Thomas: William and Theophilus died bachelors. Thomas married a daughter of John Williams, of North Wales, a chaplain in the army, and died in 1778, leaving a son, Thomas Theophilus Metcalfe, a major in the army, M.P. for Abingdon, director of the East India Company, created on 11 December 1802 Sir Thomas Theophilus Metcalfe, Bart., of Chilton, Berks." The first baronet was thus a great-grandson of the stenographer, and it is noteworthy that, since 1610, all the male members of the family have borne the name Theophilus, whilst many of the females would seem to have borne that of Theophila. The family is said to have been at one time among the most numerous in England. Metcalfe is noticed in the *D.N.B.*

———

The Penn*s* Dexterity | *By theise incomparable Contractions by which* | *a Sentence is Writt as soon as a Word* | *Allowed by Authority and past the two Univer* | *sitys with greate aprobation and aplause.* | *Invented and taught by* Ieremiah Rich *1659.*　　　　　　　　　[1111³.]

The above title is on a scroll below the portrait of Rich. Along the top border of the sheet runs the following inscription: "To the right Honourable the Lady Mary Rich. Jeremiah Rich dedicates his Penns Dexterity." At the foot of the sheet is the imprint:

Entered according to Order. And are to be sould at His house at the Golden ball in Swithins-lane.

Broadside, 16½ × 10¾ in., engraved throughout and printed on one side only, containing the alphabet, table of ideas, the Ten Commandments, Lord's

Prayer, Creed, etc. The portrait is in the top left-hand corner of the sheet. Near the bottom right-hand corner is "T: Cross sculpsit", and in the bottom right-hand corner are twelve lines of verse signed "I: R:".

This is probably the first edition of the broadside, which was entered on the Stationers' Register to Thomas Newcombe on 29 December 1658, as follows: "Master Tho. Newcomb. Entred for his copie under the hand of Master Stephens warden, one sheet of paper printed on one side called, The Pens Dexterity by these incomparable contractions by which a sentence is writt assoone as a word, allowed by authority & past the two Universities with great approbacon & applause. Invented & taught by Jeremiah Rich, the same being engraven in copper" (Roxb. *Transcript*, II, 210).

The Pepysian copy has been cut close, taking away the inscription along the top border and the imprint at the foot. Another copy of this edition, from which the portrait has been cut away, is in B.M.L. (463.h.11), the last item but one in a volume of "Various alphabets characters and inscriptions collected by Joseph Ames".

A later edition, of which there is a copy in B.L.O. (Ashm.1820ᵇ3), has the same title and date with the following imprint: "*Entered according to Order ☞ And are to be sould by Samuel Botley over against Vintners Hall in Thames street* London *and no where els*". In the bottom right-hand corner, below the twelve lines of verse signed "I: R:" is: "T. Cet I: Ch: Sculp." This edition was advertised in the Term Catalogue, Michaelmas 1673, price 2s. 6d. (*T.C.* I, 160).

Another edition, with the same title and date, is in B.M.L. (1881.c.16.(11)), the imprint at the foot of the sheet reading: "Entered according to order ☞ Sould by most Booksellers in England." With this is a letterpress key, originally pasted on the back, which has the following title: "A Key to Famous Mʳ *Rich*'s Short-hand-Table: | *Entituled,* the Pens Dexterity: *allow'd & approv'd by both* Universities. | Faithfully discovering the whole Art to the meanest Capacity (by one of his Scho- | lars) in Rich's own Method; discoursing each private Rule in its proper place, | impossible to be learnt from any spurious Pretender (already, or hereafter to be | published) designing to teach this hand. For, who can suppose, That Mr. Rich | should discover ALL his Art for Nothing, thereby hindring his Practise and his | Livelihood: No, some Secrets, or Arcanum's must be expected, and will certain- | ly be discovered to those that by a View of the Table shall be drawn to be his Scho- | lars: his Design by publishing the Table, was not to prevent Scholars from coming, | but to procure the coming of Scholars to him. And now, that so great a Piece of | Ingenuity should not be buried in Oblivion; I have presum'd, in respect to my | honored Master, to hand this KEY by it, unlocking the secrets thereof, as to dis- | cover them to Learners: and for the Truth of what I say concerning both his | Private Rules, and his Method, I appeal to all his Scholars, as fittest Judges." At the end of the "Key" is the following: "Now, Sir, in faithfulness I declare, There has nothing bin wanting save only | Mr. Rich's presence, to have multiply'd examples of each Rule, for which, | his usual price was 20s for Teaching, & 2s. 6d. his Table. Yet thy Inge- | nuity supplying that Defect, thou hast ALL; which cost every Scholar dear; | and yet not so dear, but any of them would more willingly give it again, than 2d. | for this plain Table, or any Book whatever pretending to teach it: whereby That | is a clear Truth which he published, That the Table alone was not suf- | ficient to Teach the Art; and I say it again after him; as it dos here appear. | London, Printed for the Author, and Sold by Langly Curtis in Goat Court on Ludgate Hill." Langly Curtis appears to have carried on business as a bookseller at the above address from 1668 to about 1690 (Plomer, 1668–1725, p. 96).

Another edition, $18 \times 16\frac{1}{4}$ in., in the British Museum Print Room (Cracherode coll., P.4–233), has the same title and date below the portrait, which has been re-engraved. At the top of the sheet, within a laurel border, is another title reading: "The Penns Dexterity | *More Fully Explained,* *Improved* | *and Compleated; by Adding to* | *the Two first Rules of this* | *unparralelled* Art, *wherein* | *Examples first, of the Alphabet* | *of Words to compleat that Rule* | *in the Improvement of the Vowels* | *as they are disposed about any* | *Letters. Secondly, how to Im-* | *prove the Prepositions, and the* | *Terminations, with the former* | *Rule in Long Words.* | *The want of which Rendered ẙ* | *Table very Obscure and rare if* | *attain'd without further Directions,* | *Now made usefull, and with much* | *Delight and Ease to Attaine.*"

Along the foot of the sheet is the imprint: "*Entred according to Order* ☞ *And are to be sold by William Miller at the Acorn in Sᵗ Pauls Church Yard London*, 1682." In the bottom right-hand corner of the first sheet, below the twelve lines of verse, is: "*Tho: Burnford Sc.*", and at the foot of the second sheet: "*These Examples are the same as used by Mᵗ Rich in his New Testament and Psalm Book engraven in the same* Character And by the same Hand." This edition was announced in the Term Catalogue, Michaelmas 1682 (*T.C.* I, 511).

Rich's first shorthand publication appears to have been issued in 1642 with the following title: "Semography: or, Short and Swift Writing. Being the most easiest, exactest, and speediest Method of all other that have beene yet extant: the full understanding is so easily attain'd that the Learner hereof need no other help but the book it selfe, onely which will bring him to such exactnesse that in a short time he shall be able to take word for word after the speaker with much ease. Invented and composed for the benefit of others by the Author hereof William Cartwright. And is now set forth and published by his Nephew *Ieremiah Rich* immediate next to the Authour deceased. There is divers that the Professor hereof hath taught, that will affirme this hand to outgoe all others for briefnesse, which have had the sight likewise of other hands. *All which desire to learn this hand may have the Booke to teach them. London*, Printed in the yeere, 1642." The only copy recorded is in B.M.L. (1043.b.14).

Four years later Rich published another manual of the art with the title: "Charactery or, A most Easie and Exact Method of Short and Swift Writing: Whereby *Sermons* or *Speeches* may be Exactly taken, Word for Word from the mouth of the Speaker with much ease and speed. The full understanding of this Art is easily attained in one Weeks time, by the help of this Book only. Invented and exactly Composed by Jeremiah Rich, Teacher of the said Art in Sᵗ *Olives* Parish in *Southwark*, at one Mʳⁱˢ. *Williams* a Mid-wife. *London*, Printed by Peter Cole at the sign of the *Printing presse* in Cornhil neer the Royal Exchange, 1646." This work was entered on the Stationers' Register to Peter Cole on 4 September 1646 (Roxb. *Transcript*, I, 244). The only copy known, formerly in the collection of Dr William Blair, is now in L.C.W. (A56.R5 C-Office). Another shorthand treatise by Rich appeared in 1654 with the following title: "Semigraphy: or, Arts Rarity. As it hath been proved by many honourable Persons, and allowed by the Learned, To be the easiest, exactest, and briefest Method of short and swift writing as ever was yet known; So that by the help of this Book, and halfe an houres practise with the Author, an ordinary Capacity may attain the full knowledge thereof. Invented, exactly composed, and (after many yeares practice therein) is now sent abroad to benefit the World, By Jeremiah Rich, Author and Teacher thereof, dwelling at *S. Olaves* in *Southwarke* in *Mill-Lane*. *Every good and perfect gift comes from God. London*, Printed by *J. G.* and are to be sold by *N. Brook* at the *Angel* in *Corne-Hill*. 1654." This book has an engraved title by Thomas Cross (Johnson, No. 17) and a frontispiece portrait of the author. It was entered on the Stationers' Register to Nathaniel Brook on 15 April 1654 (Roxb. *Transcript*, I, 446). The only known copies are in B.M.L. (1043.b.55); N.L.S. (Warden coll., Wn.856); and C.E.B. (Havette coll.).

After Rich's death his system was published under the title "The Pens Dexterity Compleated". The first edition of this work was entered on the Stationers' Register to Henry Eversden on 24 March 1668–9 (Roxb. *Transcript*, II, 398) and was announced in the Term Catalogue, Trinity 1669. Copies are in B.M.L. (1043.b.56); B.L.O. (Ashmole A.27, wanting portrait); C.L.M. (Harland coll., Mun.D.1.85, wanting portrait); R.L.M. (Bailey coll., 514.K.43); B.G.P. (Guénin coll., Δ68502, Réserve); and W.J.C. (O'Donnell coll.). An edition was announced in the Term Catalogue, Trinity 1674 (*T.C.* I, 182). A copy with this date, called the third edition, is in W.J.C. Copies of the fourth edition, 1676, are in U.L.C. (L.32.56³) and N.L.S. (Warden coll., Wn.851). The fifth edition, 1682, was announced in the Term Catalogue, Trinity 1680 (*T.C.* I, 409). Copies are in L.N.Y. (Beale coll., *IDS p.v. 74, no. 2); U.L.Y. (Healey coll., F25.335); and W.J.C. The sixth edition, 1713, is in R.L.M. (Bailey coll., 514.K.44) and W.J.C. A copy of the seventh edition, without date, is in R.L.M. (Bailey coll., 514.K.45). There were many later editions, the last being apparently the twentieth, printed at Leeds in 1792.

In addition to his broadside and books of instruction Rich was responsible for two publications engraved in his shorthand, the Book of Psalms and the New Testament, neither of which is in the Pepysian Library. The first edition of the Psalms bears the following title: "The Whole Book of Psalms in Meter *According to the* Art of Short-writing written by Jeremiah Rich *Author and Teacher of the said Art* London Printed *for the Author and are to be sould at his house the Golden Ball in Swithins Lane neare London Stone.*" This tiny volume, which measures only 2½ × 1½ in., was engraved by Thomas Cross and has a frontispiece portrait of Rich. It is undated, but may be assigned to about 1660 and may well be the work alluded to in the Diary on 16 April 1661, when Pepys "found Mr. Coventry reading of the Psalms in short hand (which he is now busy about), and had good sport about the long marks that are made there for sentences in divinity which he is never like to make use of". Copies of the first edition are in B.M.L. (G.11659 and C.18.a.33.(2), bound with the New Testament, Eversden ed.); B.L.O. (Arch.Bodl.A.1.108.I.6); R.L.M. (Bailey coll., 514.K.42); N.L.S. (Warden coll., Wn.913); L.N.Y. (*KVM); and W.J.C.

A posthumous edition was announced in the Term Catalogue, Michaelmas 1673, price 5*s*. (*T.C.* 1, 160). The imprint of this edition reads: "London Printed *and are sold by Samuel Botley teacher of the said Art over against Vintners Hall in Thames streete, and no where els*". Copies are in B.M.L. (600.i.23/33.(2), bound with the New Testament); R.L.M. (Bailey coll., 514.K.42); N.L.S. (Warden coll., Wn.915); The Library, Armagh, Ireland; L.N.Y. (*KVM); and W.J.C.

Another edition has the imprint: "London Printed *and sold by Samuel Botley teacher of the said Art at Colonel Masons Coffee house in Cornhill.*" Its date is probably about 1675. A copy is in W.J.C.

The last known edition of Rich's Book of Psalms bears the imprint: "London Printed *for Wm Marshall at y̆ bible in Newgate streete & Jn° Marshall at y̆ bible in gracechurch streete nere Cornehill y̆ twentieth Impresion*". A copy is in W.J.C. (O'Donnell coll.).

The publication of Rich's Psalms was followed by that of the New Testament, in a volume of the same height and width but more than twice its bulk, engraved throughout by Thomas Cross, with the same portrait of Rich prefixed. Like the Psalms, it is undated, but internal evidence suggests that it was printed in 1666 or 1667. The title of the first edition reads: "The Book of the New Testament of our Lord and Saviour Jesus Christ according to the art of short writing invented and taught by Jeremiah Rich London *Printed for the Authour And are to be sold by Henry Eversden under the Crown Tavern in West-Smithfield*". With the exception of the author's name and the imprint, this title is in shorthand. The names of forty-one subscribers are printed on the last four pages of the book.

Copies of the first edition are in B.M.L. (C.18.a.33.(1), lacking the portrait, bound with the Psalms, 1st ed.); B.L.O. (Aubrey, 32); British & Foreign Bible Society, London (H.C.529, wanting title-page); B.L.M.; L.N.Y. (Beale and Rockwell colls., *KVM); U.L.Y. (Healey coll., X 373 M 659); and W.J.C.

A posthumous edition, announced in the Term Catalogue, Michaelmas 1673, has the imprint: "London *Printed and are sold by Samuel Botley teacher of ẙ said art over against Vintners Hall in Thames street and no where els*". The last four pages contain the names of forty-five subscribers, including Samuel Botley. The volume was sold singly for 10*s*. or bound with the Psalms for 15*s*. (*T.C.* 1, 160). Copies are in the B.M.L. (600.i.23/33.(1), bound with the Psalms); N.L.S. (Warden coll., Wn.915, bound with the Psalms); L.N.Y. (Beale and Howard colls., *KVM); and W.J.C. (J. E. Hodgkin's copy, as to which see *Notes and Queries*, 6th ser., XI, 76).

Another edition, issued probably about 1675, has the imprint: "London Printed *and are to be sold by Samuel Botley teacher of ẙ said art at Colonel Mason's Coffee house in Cornhill.*" Copies are in the University Library, Basle (AN.v.19); L.N.Y. (*KVM); J.R.G.; and W.J.C.

The New Testament and Psalms were announced in the Term Catalogue, Easter 1693, as "newly reprinted, to be sold either bound together, or singly: wrought off upon fine paper. Printed for R. Clavell at the Peacock in St. Paul's Churchyard" (*T.C.* II, 458). No copy with such an imprint has been located.

Another edition, announced as "reprinted" in the Term Catalogue, Trinity 1697, has the imprint: "London *Printed for Wᵐ Marshall at ẙ Bible in* *newgate street & J^{no}, Marshall at ŷ Bible in gracechurch streete nere Cornehill ŷ twentieth Impression"*. The New Testament was to be had "bound for 6s. alone; with the Psalms bound with it, 8s." (*T.C.* III, 9, 30). Copies of this edition are in B.M.L. (C.o.d.3); British & Foreign Bible Society, London (H.C.676); R.L.M. (Bailey coll., 514.K.42); P.L.L.; L.N.Y. (Beale coll.); and W.J.C.

Another issue was announced in the Term Catalogue, Michaelmas 1703, as "printed for J. Marshall at the Bible in Grace-Church street" (*T.C.* III, 377).

The dedication to the Duke of Buckingham and seven other "honoured freinds", which originally appeared in the Book of Psalms, is found in some copies of the New Testament.

Rich's shorthand alphabet, although embodying many of the characters of Edmond Willis and Shelton, represented a distinct advance on those of his precursors. The superfluous letter *c* was discarded, *g* and *j* were expressed by the same sign, *a* and *t* by the stroke / written in different directions. A noteworthy innovation was the representation of two related sounds (*m* and *n*, *k* and *x*) by one stroke differing only in length—a device which many modern system-makers have exploited to the full. Rich reduced the vowel places from five to four, *e* being usually omitted or expressed by a small circle which provided a natural junction for the preceding and following consonants. The use of this expedient—the first attempt at joined vowels— was, however, restricted by the fact that a circle formed an integral part of certain consonants (*p*, *q*, *r*). The other vowels were also omitted frequently in the body of a word with advantage to speed if not to legibility. The indica- tion of initial *i* by a dot was a tentative step towards the elaborate vocalisation schemes of later authors who relied on disjoined dots, dashes or commas for the expression of all the vowel sounds. Rich appears to have been the first to substitute the single stroke \ for the compound V for *v*, an improvement which was not without influence on the subsequent development of shorthand system construction. Diphthongs were dismissed with the remark: "There is no use in this art either of diphthongs or double vowels: the intent of the practice of short and swift writing aiming only at sounds of words, not the truth of spelling." The regular formation of words by alphabetical characters was a feature of the system which has been obscured by Rich's lavish use of arbitrary contractions (many of which display no little ingenuity) for the representation of theological phrases.

Rich's shorthand was extensively practised for nearly two centuries, among others by John Locke, who recommended it in his essay "On Education" as "the best contrived of any I have seen", and Dr Philip Doddridge, who introduced it into the curriculum of his nonconformist academy at Northampton and printed his own version of it in 1799. An edition of the system was published as late as 1830.

JEREMIAH RICH (1630?–1667?), one of the most famous stenographers of the seventeenth century, was a man of action as well as a versatile writer and poet. The date of his birth is not known, but it can hardly have been later than 1630. A crudely engraved portrait in the British Museum (P.R.) gives his age as 24, and Bromley's "Catalogue of Engraved British Portraits" (1793) states that such a portrait was prefixed to Rich's "Pen's Dexterity", 1659; but this would make him a boy of seven years when his name appeared on the title-page of "Semography" in 1642. The system of shorthand expounded in that book is said to have been "invented and composed...by the author hereof William Cartwright, and is now set forth and published by his Nephew Ieremiah Rich immediate next to the Authour deceased". In the preface to the same work Rich declares: "Although I am not father to it, yet am I the right heire, for my Uncle dying left it to me only." The portrait by Cross prefixed to Rich's "Semigraphy", 1654, seems to be that of a young man of 20 or thereabouts.

In 1642 or 1643 Rich was engaged, apparently in some clerical capacity, in the service of the Parliament whose cause he had espoused, and five or six years later he was attached to the military forces opposed to Charles I. He was perhaps the Mr Rich who in June 1650 was directed to send to the Lord President of the Council copies of examinations taken by him in relation to the suppression of unlicensed printers and vendors of books in Leicestershire (*State Papers, Domestic Series: Council of State Order Books*, vol. IX). In 1646, as the title-page of his "Charactery" indicates, he was living at the house of Mistress Williams, a mid-wife, in St Olave's parish, Southwark, where he taught a shorthand system of which he claimed to be the inventor, omitting all mention of his uncle Cartwright. Colonel Nathaniel Rich had raised a troop of horse in Essex as early as 1643, with which he joined the Earl of Manchester's army. Early in 1648 the colonel and his troop marched through the city into Southwark, and Jeremiah Rich probably accompanied him during the campaign which resulted in the recapture of Dover, Walmer, Deal and Sandown for the Parliament in the summer of that year. In 1648 he published "Jeremiah's Contemplations on Jeremiah's Lamentations, or England's Miseries Matcht with Sion's Elegies", a work of which the contents can only be inferred from its title, since no copy is known to be extant. His name is also found appended to a broadside "Elegie on the Death of the Right Honourable Iohn Warner, late Lord Mayor of London", published on 13 November 1648. Rich's next book, "Mellificium Musarum: the Marrow of the Muses. Or an Epitome of Divine Poetry", appeared in 1650, with a dedication to "my Noble Colonell, Nathaniel Rich", in which he observed that "it is requisite I should sometimes waite on your Honour with my Pen, as well as alwaies with my sword".

A year or two after his period of active service with the army, Rich was appointed Clerk of the Check on board the frigate "Portland", under Captain William Rouse. In that capacity he took part in the decisive naval battle with the Dutch, in July 1653, off the coast of Holland, in the course of which Rouse received injuries from which he died three months later and the Dutch admiral Tromp was among the killed, as was the Clerk of the Check on another British vessel. Rich must have returned to London immediately afterwards, for on 20 August he recorded the proceedings at the trial of the notorious pamphleteer, John Lilburn. In the preface to "Semigraphy" a number of his admirers testified that "the grand triall of Mr. John Lilbourn at the Old Baily" had been "exactly taken by Mr. Rich". The same claim was made in a small poster advertising the book, which stated that "the Author does ordinarily write a Sermon in less then the Sixteenth part of a sheet of Paper, folded up in the bredth of a two pence, and dare undertake with such a Book as the most Short-hand Writers use, to take a Sermon with both his eyes blinded, and not miss. He also wrote a Sermon in little more then the Two and thirtieth part of a sheet of Paper, in a Book containing the breadth of a single penny, being now shown in the Publick library in Oxford, which is a mystery to the World, and was never done by any but himself, since the use of a Pen was known." The smallest MS. in the Bodleian Library was identified in 1912 by A. Tremaine Wright as being the sermon here referred to (*Notes and Queries*, 11 ser. VI, 345, 2 Nov. 1912). It has been exhibited there, attached to its original chain, for many years.

In July 1654 Rich submitted letters of recommendation from "several persons of honour and integrity" in support of his petition to the Committee of the Admiralty for further employment in the navy. In this document he alluded to his services to the Commonwealth extending over eleven years and to "those many difficulties and dangers, sicknesses and sorrows your petitioner hath suffered by sea and land in the late wars, his life having been a continual tragedy while he hath sailed through this red sea of sorrow in the midst of the valley of Achor." One of the letters was from Colonel Nathaniel Rich, certifying that the bearer had served for two years and a quarter under his command "and in all that time behaved himself faithfully and valiantly".

Soon afterwards Rich was stricken by a serious illness which prompted his next publication, "The Mirrour of Mercy in the Midst of Misery: or Life triumphant in Death, wherein Free-will is abolished and Free-grace exalted....Written in a fit of Sicknesse, by Jeremiah Rich", 1654. No copy of this book, which was apparently in verse, is known to have survived. In the same year appeared a new shorthand manual entitled "Semigraphy: or, Arts Rarity...by Jeremiah Rich, author and teacher thereof, dwelling at S. Olaves in Southwarke in Mill-Lane." "It is not long since I was at the doore of death", he writes in the dedication to Lady Mary Rich, who became Duchess of Warwick in 1659, and he reveals that Lady Mary had spent "some houres" in studying his shorthand "when I was in the family".

At some date which must have been subsequent to the publication of "Semigraphy" Rich left his abode in Southwark and took a house in St Swithin's Lane, at the sign of the Golden Ball, where he gave instruction in shorthand daily from 8 to 4. From this address Rich sent out the poster to which reference has been made and, in 1659, an engraved broadside entitled "The Penns Dexterity", also dedicated to Lady Mary Rich, displaying the system without explanatory text. The reaction which set in soon after the death of Cromwell in September 1658 and the imminent restoration of the monarchy must have given Rich, as one who had been actively associated with the dominant party in the Commonwealth, food for serious reflection. The outcome was the publication of another broadside entitled "Logomachia: A Harmony in Discord, shewing the mutual submission of the Episcopal party in the City, and the Independent Souldiery, to Charles, by the Grace of God, King of England, Scotland, France, & Ireland, Defender of the Faith." This attempt to reconcile the trend of events with his own convictions took the form of a dialogue in verse between the city and a soldier and, although undated, belongs evidently to the spring of 1660. It was probably about this time that Rich undertook the writing of Sternhold and Hopkins's metrical version of the Psalms in his short-hand, engraved by Thomas Cross and sold at the author's house, the Golden Ball, in Swithin's Lane near London Stone. The fact that the dedication to the Duke of Buckingham and others is not found in some copies of the first edition suggests that it was added after the Restoration.

Jeremiah Rich seems to have excelled in microscopic penmanship. According to William Leybourn's "Pleasure with Profit" (1694) he took down a sermon delivered by a bishop at Whitehall before Charles II. After testifying to its accuracy, the bishop requested him to present a specimen of his art to the king. Thereupon Rich "wrote the same Sermon in a little Book of Six Leaves of Fine Paper, and had it bound in Crimson Sarcenet, with Silver Clasps and Corners upon the Cover; all which Book and Cover was less than the nail of his little Finger; which Book he afterwards presented to the King".

For reasons which can only be conjectured, Rich seems to have quitted the metropolis for a time. On 23 November 1663 he produced his authority to teach shorthand at Reading (*Hist. MSS. Com., Report II, App. VII*, p. 195), but he was probably back in London by the summer of 1664, when news of the death of Lord Rutherford, Governor of Tangier, in an encounter with the Moors, provoked another broadside elegy from his pen: "Death's Envious Triumph; in a Brief Memorial of the Losse of the Late Incomparable and Excellent Andrew, Lord Rutherford Earle of Teveot, &c. Killed by an Ambuscadoe of Moores, May 3d, 1664." The reception accorded to his "Book of Psalms" may have encouraged him to undertake the more ambitious task of writing the New Testament in shorthand. It was engraved, like the Psalms, by Cross, and the date of its publication was probably about 1666 when, as internal evidence shows, the address to the subscribers was written.

Rich did not long survive the publication of his "New Testament", and although the exact date of his death has not been ascertained, it must have taken place before the middle of 1669. In June of that year appeared "The Pens Dexterity Compleated: or, Mr. Riches Short-hand now perfectly Taught, Which in his Life-time was never done, by any thing made publique in Print, because it would have hindred his Practice." This title and an allusion on page 31 to "our deceased Author" prove conclusively that Rich was then in his grave. Certain bequests were made to the Free School in Old Jewry by a Mr Rich, who had been a writing master at the school (Hatton's *New View of London*, 1708, p. 705) and may possibly have been Jeremiah Rich. One of the specimens of penmanship in the Pepysian "calligraphical collection" (vol. III, p. 252) is by "Mr Rich, Writing M^r in London".

(A. T. Wright's *Jeremiah Rich*, 1911; Sir Ambrose Heal's *The English Writing-Masters and their Copy-Books*, 1931, pp. 87–8; *Phonetic Journal*, XLV, 146–8, 27 March 1886; *Pitman's Journal*, LXV, 185–6, 10 March 1906; *Notes and Queries*, CLXXII, 42.)

Stenographie: | or, | The Art of *Short-Writing*. | Composed in a more brief, plain, | and easie way, then hitherto hath | been published. | By which Art, Sermons, Speeches, or | the like, may be taken word for word, | with very little or no charge | to memory. | *By* Tho: Heath. | Psal. 45. 2. | *My tongue is the pen of a ready writer.* | Lypsius. | *Scripturæ compendium, cum verba non perscribi-* | *mus, sed signamus.* | Imprimatur, *John Downame.* | [Woodcut of a hand holding a pen which has traced in a notebook the shorthand characters: ʌ ʔ ᴗ ſ ꝺ ᴔ ꝫ ᴖ ꝯ ʟ ſ o ʒ] | *London,* | Printed in the Yeere, 1644. [402⁷.]

5⅝ × 3⅜ in., pp. (4) + 16 letterpress. No headlines to pages. The shorthand characters are engraved. Sign. (A1–2), B–B8.

Leaf 1ᵃ Title, 1ᵇ blank, 2ᵃ–2ᵇ To the Reader, 3ᵃ–10ᵇ Text of "Short-Writing".

The Pepysian copy is the only one recorded. In B.L.O. (8° P.31.Art.Bs) is a unique copy of a later edition, with the following title: "Stenography, | Or the Art of | *Short-Writing:* | More Easy and Plain than | formerly hath been Extant, | with | Examples and Observations, which | will help the Learner so as he needeth | no help but the Book. | Published by the Author

Tho. Heath | Stationer. | *Honos alit Artes.* | London, | Printed and sold by the Author at the | *Globe* within *Ludgate* 1664" (6½ × 4 in., pp. 16 letterpress and 16 engraved plates printed on one side). At the foot of the last page is engraved: "Imprimatur May 19: 1664 Roger L'estrange."

In the preface to the 1664 edition the author refers to "a Former Piece of Art, which I published above twenty years agoe", and adds: "My last book being now by most, neer out of Memory, I shall in this blow up its Sparkes."

The influence of Shelton's "Tachygraphy" is clearly visible in Heath's shorthand alphabet, though he interchanged the signs for *b* and *n*, and modified those for *a* and *w*, while reinstating Edmond Willis's symbol for *s*.

THOMAS HEATH (fl. 1634–1664), a London bookseller, was living in Russell Street, Covent Garden, "near the Piazza", from 1651 to 1655. In 1651 his imprint is found on "A Continuation of Sir Philip Sidney's Arcadia", and he issued several plays, most of which were printed for him by Thomas Newcomb. In 1655 he published "Theophania: Or severall Modern Histories Represented by way of Romance", with a preface by himself. Heath was established in 1664 at the Globe on Ludgate Hill, whence he issued a halfpenny token, now very scarce. It bore his own and his wife's initials, as well as a representation of his sign, a globe on a stand. In "The Newes", No. 49, 20 June 1664, Heath's second shorthand treatise is announced as follows:

"*Stenography*, or the Art of Short-Writing made both plain, and easy with Examples and Observations. Sold and Composed by *Tho. Heath* Stationer within *Ludgate*, where you may also have Scriveners Labels."

In the preface to the above work he stated that he had written shorthand "near thirty years" and was contemplating the publication of a treatise on arithmetic. He acknowledged his indebtedness to previous writers on stenography, mentioning Willis and Metcalfe "and many others, which hath rung their fame throughout the world"; but considered that Shelton's first system was then one of the best extant.

The date of Heath's death has not been ascertained, but he had been succeeded at the Globe on Ludgate Hill by C. Brown before 1707 (*London Topographical Record*, 1903, II, 88).

Short-Writing | Shortned: | or, | The Art of Short-writing | reduced
to a Method more spee- | dy, plain, exact, and easie, than | hath
been heretofore Published. | In which, | The principal Difficulties
and Discou- | ragements that have been found in Short- | writing,
particularly the buthening of me- | mory with, and inconvenient
joyning of | many Characters, are removed; And | the whole Art so
disposed, that all | usual words may be written with | aptnesse and
brevity. | By John Farthing late Author and | Teacher thereof, who
had practised Short- | writing 46. years. | *London*: | Printed for
Tho. Parkhurst, at the *Bible* and *Three-* | *Crowns* in *Cheapside* near
Mercers-Chappel. 1684.   [860 9.]

6½ × 3¾ in., 8vo, pp. (10) letterpress, 9 engraved leaves printed on both
sides, 1 engraved leaf printed on recto only, pp. 6 (numbered 33–8). With
headlines. Sign. A–(A7). Shorthand characters in the text engraved on wood.
The plates were engraved by Thomas Cross, whose name appears at the
foot of leaf 6ᵃ.

Leaf 1ᵃ Title, 1ᵇ blank, 2ᵃ–2ᵇ "To the reader desirous to learn short-
writing" signed by ten divines, 3ᵃ–5ᵇ "To the reader.... From my house in
Olaves-street in Southwark, March 1, 1653", 6ᵃ The Lords Prayer, Creed,
Ten Commandments, and St John's Gospel Chap. xvi in shorthand,
6ᵇ Alphabet, 7ᵃ Chap. 1 Of the alphabet of letters, 7ᵇ Double consonants,
8ᵃ Chap. 2 Of the double consonants, 8ᵇ–10ᵃ Chap. 3 Of the vowels and
their places, Chap. 4 Of the use of the vowel places, 10ᵇ Characters for
shortning of words, 11ᵃ–11ᵇ Chap. V Of the characters for shortning of
words, 12ᵃ Characters for the names of the bookes of the Bible, 12ᵇ–15ᵃ The
table of words, 15ᵇ blank, 16ᵃ Chap. VI Of the table of words, 16ᵇ–18ᵃ
Chap. VII General rules for shortning of words, 18ᵇ Chap. VIII Of
pointing. Finis.

This is a posthumous edition of Farthing's shorthand system, first published
in 1654. Other copies are in B.L.O. (302.g.148), B.M.L. (G.16758.(1)),
C.L.W., N.L.S. (Warden coll., Wn.829) and W.J.C. In some of these the
second word of the title is printed "Shotned". The Bodleian, N.L.S.,
Crawford and Carlton copies contain no preliminary letterpress. The

Bodleian and N.L.S. copies have 8 additional letterpress pages of "Books Printed for and Sold by John Marshall, at the Bible in Gracechurch-street", with the signatures G–G4, showing this to have been a later issue (about 1700?).

The first edition of Farthing's "Short-writing shortned" was entered on the Stationers' Register to Thomas Underhill on 25 March 1654 (Roxb. *Transcript*, I, 444). The only copies recorded are in C.L.M. (formerly John Byrom's, Harland coll., Mun.D1.39); L.C.W. (Z56.F25, lacking the engraved leaf containing the Lord's Prayer, etc., and leaf 11 containing Chapter V of the text); L.N.Y. (*KC1654). The title is as above, with slight variations of spelling and punctuation, down to "brevity". Then follows: "By John Farthing Authour and Teacher thereof, who wrote Mr *Christopher Love's* Trial and hath practised Short-writing this 26. years. *London*, Printed for *Tho. Vnderhill*, and are to be sold at the Blew Anchor in *Pauls* Church-yard, and by the Authour at his House in *Olaves*-street in *Southwark*, and at his Chamber in the House that was Alderman *Freemans* in *Cornhill*, near the Royall Exchange. 1654." This edition contains also an engraved title by Thomas Cross, dated 1654.

Another edition, with the letterpress title-page of 1654 and the engraved title-page dated 1662, is in C.L.M. (Harland coll., Mun.D1.85). The last three lines, excepting the date, have been crossed through in ink.

Farthing's system has few original features, although he anticipated Mason, Blanchard, Pitman and others by introducing a small circle to represent *s*. He claimed to have reduced the list of contractions for prefixes and suffixes to a lesser number than any of his predecessors.

JOHN FARTHING (fl. 1620–1674) is known to have been living in "Olaves-street in Southwark" in March 1653/4, when he claimed to have had 26 years' experience as a shorthand writer. This information is derived from his "Short-Writing Shortned", the title-page of which also informs us that he had at that date "a Chamber in the House that was Alderman Freeman's [i.e. Sir Ralph Freeman, Lord Mayor of London] in Cornhill, near the Royal Exchange". He was possibly the John Farthing, cordwainer, whose eldest son John, born in the parish of St Olave, Southwark, on 16 May 1635, was admitted to the Merchant Taylors' School in 1648 (Robinson's *Register*, 1, 187). The registers of St Olave record the baptisms and burials of several other children of this John Farthing between 1640 and 1645.

Farthing was writing and teaching shorthand in the spring of 1641. Five sermons preached by Jeremiah Burroughs in March and April of that year were printed in 1654 in a volume entitled "The Saints Treasury", with a preface signed by six divines testifying that they had been "very happily taken" by "Master Farthing, now a teacher of Short-writing; one who hath given ample testimony of his great skill and dexterity in writing Short-hand".

Thomas Hawes, a neighbour of Farthing's in St Olave's parish, was arrested in March 1645/6 on a charge of blasphemy and imprisoned in Winchester House, Southwark. J. Westby Gibson (*Bibliography of Shorthand*, 1887, p. 65) states that Hawes's trial was taken down by Farthing, but gives no authority. In a pamphlet entitled "The Afflicted Christian Justifyed", issued in vindication of Hawes two months after his arrest, Farthing is held up to reprobation for his "Arbitrary Insolencies, and High Commission proceedings against the native Freedoms and Birthrights of the whole Free-borne People of England", and in "A Christian Relation of a Christian's Affliction", published in March 1646/7, Hawes accused John Farthing, "stuffe weaver in St. Olaves parish", of being the chief instigator of the proceedings against him.

The trial of the Rev. Christopher Love in Westminster Hall for high treason, which caused some stir in June 1651, was reported by Farthing on behalf of the accused. Love was convicted of plotting against the Commonwealth. The trial, "printed by exact Copies of those who took it in Short-hand", was first published in 1652. At the Restoration it was re-issued with a new title-page, bearing the name of "John Farthing, Citizen of London, who took the Triall in the said Court in Short-writing for Mr. Love, and at his own request". In an address to the reader Farthing wrote: "This triall was formerly printed, but not till now made thus publick, the times not bearing it. The Court took a severe course to have prevented the publishing of it, as being (it seems) conscious to themselves of their own foul and false play therein; and did therefore every day commit my very Notes to the Tower, (though they did not prove to be under such strong keeping, but that I had the liberty of giving them severall visits)." From the speech of the Attorney-General, it appears that the shorthand writer sat next to the prisoner in court. Love's speech and prayer on the scaffold on Tower Hill were reported independently by Farthing and another shorthand writer, John Hinde. A comparison of the two reports shows that while Hinde's was rather fuller, Farthing's was the more carefully edited.

The fact that the title-page of the 1684 edition of Farthing's "Short-Writing Shortned" refers to the "late" author's 46 years' experience as a shorthand writer, as compared with the 26 years of the 1654 edition, seems to warrant the inference that his death took place about 1674.

An | Epitome | of | *Stenographie;* | or, | An Abridgement and Contraction, of | the Art of short, swift, and secret Writing by Cha- | racters, both fair, lineall, and legible, as will | appear here-after, as well as in the | *Prefixt Example.* | Being a brief, yet plain and full dis- | covery of all the Grounds of the whole Art: In its | several Examples, Rules, Wayes, Formes, Methods | and Kindes of Abreviation, and Contraction of | *Words, Clauses, and Sentences:* By which, (without | the Help of any Tutor, Teacher or School-master) | the weakest Capacities may with ease and speed, at- | tain unto the Perfect Knowledge and Practice there- | of, even in this its present swift, short, succinct, a- | bridged and contracted Form. | A work of very great use and advantage also, for *the Fur-* | *ther Perfecting* of all those who have already for many | yeares together practised this Art, in the other seve- | rall Forms of it. | *Written by* Job Everardt. | Printed by *M. S.* for *Lodowick Lloyd,* and are to be sold | at his Shop, next to the *Castle-Tavern* in *Cornhil,* 1658.

[402 ¹².]

5¾ × 3½ in., 8vo, pp. (24) letterpress + 25 engraved plates (numbered 1 to 25) printed on one side + 64 pp. letterpress (numbered 27 to 90) + 1 p. With headlines. Sign. A8, (B4), C–F8 in eights. Prefixed to the letterpress title-page is an engraved title-page reading as follows:

An | Epitome | of | Stenography | or | *an Abridgement and* | *Contraction* *of the* | *Art of* Short, | *Swift, and* Secret-*Writing* | *by* Characters | By | Job: | Eueerardt

Leaf 1ᵃ–1ᵇ blank, 2ᵃ blank, 2ᵇ Acrostic, 3ᵃ Engraved title, 3ᵇ "Prefixt example", 4ᵃ Printed title, 4ᵇ Shorthand specimens in thirty-three languages,

5ᵃ–6ᵇ Transcription of shorthand specimens, 7ᵃ–9ᵇ Dedication to Sir John Davie, Bt., and others, 10ᵃ–10ᵇ Verses on "The excellency and utility of this art", 11ᵃ–12ᵃ "The Direction for the learning of this Art", 12ᵇ–13ᵃ blank, 13ᵇ Errata and "An Advertisement of Remarque", 14ᵃ blank, 14ᵇ–15ᵃ Alphabet, prefixes and terminations, 15ᵇ–16ᵃ blank, 16ᵇ–17ᵃ Prefixes, terminations and contractions, 17ᵇ–18ᵃ blank, 18ᵇ–19ᵃ Contractions, 19ᵇ–20ᵃ blank, 20ᵇ–21ᵃ Contractions, 21ᵇ–22ᵃ blank, 22ᵇ Contractions, 23ᵃ Contractions of phrases, 23ᵇ–24ᵃ blank, 24ᵇ–25ᵃ Contractions and diphthongs, 25ᵇ–26ᵃ blank, 26ᵇ–27ᵃ Examples, 27ᵇ–28ᵃ blank, 28ᵇ–29ᵃ Examples, 29ᵇ–30ᵃ blank, 30ᵇ–31ᵃ Contractions of words, 31ᵇ–32ᵃ blank, 32ᵇ–33ᵃ Examples, 33ᵇ–34ᵃ blank, 34ᵇ–35ᵃ Examples and contractions of phrases, 35ᵇ–36ᵃ blank, 36ᵇ–37ᵃ Contractions of phrases, 37ᵇ blank, 38ᵃ Contractions with "Iob: Everardt" at foot, 38ᵇ blank, 39ᵃ–70ᵇ Text.

The Pepysian copy lacks the leaf containing the acrostic. Other copies are in B.M.L. (7942.a.22, with a note: "The only perfect copy I have met with", signed William Blair, July 1812; E.1845.(1), lacking the leaf with acrostic); B.L.O. (Bliss A.80); C.L.M. (Harland coll., Mun.D.1.57); N.L.S. (Warden coll., Wn.828); I.S.W.; C.L.W.; P.L.L. (lacking all after p. 76); L.C.W. (Bindley and Hanbury colls., Z56.E91); N.Y.L. (Beale coll., Reserve); U.L.Y. (Healey coll., F25.342, lacking engraved title-page); C.E.B. (Havette coll.); and W.J.C. On the recto of the first leaf (1ᵃ) of the copy in R.L.M. (Bailey coll., 514.G.53) is printed: "For the Worshipfull and the Truly Honoured Mʳˢ. Lydia Martin, in Clarkenwell-Close, London", within a border of typographical ornaments. The copy in C.E.B. has a similar printed dedication to "Mrs. Margaret Davie, at Credy, neere Crediton, in Devon." In the later impressions the errata listed on 13ᵇ are corrected.

Everardt acknowledges that his work is a synthesis of various published systems, "with some others which were never yet printed". His alphabet includes a large proportion of compound characters and alternative signs for *a*, *s*, *t* and *u*. Among other devices, he advocates writing certain words by "significants", literal significants consisting of the first or last letters of the word, symbolical significants "such as have a Resemblance, or Reason in the very Form and Figure of them, of what they signifie". Curious features of the book are an ingenious rhyming triple acrostic and, in place of the usual specimen of the Ten Commandments, Lord's Prayer and Creed, a sentence from Habbakuk in thirty-three languages, in shorthand and longhand. Lewis's verdict on the work is severe: "As for the book of Job Everardt, it would require the patience of Job himself to read his work a second time, or to study its instructions. . . . How any man could sit down deliberately to write a system of shorthand, and not by mere accident produce something better, is utterly incomprehensible!" (*Historical Account of the Rise and Progress of Short Hand*, pp. 72–4.)

No biographical particulars of Job Everardt have been recovered.

Stenographie | and | *Crytographie:* | or the | Arts of Short | and | Secret Writing. | The first laid down in a | method familiar to meane | Capacities: | The second added to convince | and cautionate the credulous and | the confident, and to Exercise and | humour the ingenious and | their fancies. | By N. B.— | *Omne bonum Dei donum.* | *London,* | Printed by *J. G.* for the Author, and are | to be had at his house in *Putney* in the | County of *Surrey.* 1659.

[402².]

5⅝ × 3⅜ in., 8vo, engraved portrait, pp. (12)+68 letterpress+24 engraved plates (numbered 1 to 23) printed on one side. With headlines. Sign. A–E7 in eights. Pp. 54–66 are also paged separately 1–10.

Leaf 1ᵃ blank, 1ᵇ Portrait of Bridges by D. Loggan with 2 lines below, 2ᵃ Title within border of printer's ornaments, 2ᵇ blank, 3ᵃ Dedication to Sir Orlando Bridgman, 3ᵇ blank, 4ᵃ–5ᵇ To the Reader, "March ⁵⁸⁄₅₉ the first of the 4. last months of 13. yeares squandered in the Valley of Fortune", 6ᵃ–7ᵃ In Commendation of Fair Writing, 7ᵇ blank, 8ᵃ–19ᵃ Text of Stenographie, 19ᵇ–41ᵇ Text of Cryptographie (incl. a leaf without pagination between pp. 54 and 55). Engraved plates numbered 1–23 printed on recto only, containing alphabet, double consonants, abbreviations for words and sentences, etc. The last leaf, not numbered, engraved on recto only, contains the Lord's Prayer, the Creed and the Ten Commandments in shorthand.

This is the first edition. It was entered on the Stationers' Register to John Grismond, the printer, on 30 January 1659–60 (Roxb. *Transcript,* II, 248) "in trust for the author Mr Bridges aforesaid". The author's full name, Noah Bridges, appears on the leaf of dedication and in the Stationers' Register.

The Pepysian copy lacks the portrait, but contains the leaf between pp. 54 and 55. In the Pepysian copy the engraved plates are bound between "In Commendation of Fair Writing" and p. 1 of the text.

Other copies are in B.M.L. (7942.a.28, with bookplate of H. Walpole, wanting portrait); B.L.O. (25788.f.22, wanting portrait); U.L.C. (L.32.59^2, wanting portrait); C.C.O. ("Ex dono Revd. Joshua Reynolds, S.T.B.", W.K.8.12); R.L.M. (Bailey coll., 514.G.10, "Ed. Stearne habet Ex dono Authoris 1659"); C.L.M. (Harland coll., Mun.D2.5, wanting portrait); C.L.W. (wanting portrait); L.C.W. (wanting portrait); L.N.Y. (Beale coll., *KC(1659)); Watkinson Library, Hartford, Conn.; P.L.L. (O'Donnell coll.); and W.J.C. A variant issue, the plates having been re-engraved, is in W.J.C.

The second edition is known only from Kennett's *Register and Chronicle*, 1728, i. 655, where it is described as follows under the date March 1662: "Stenography and Cryptography. The Arts of short and secret Writing. The second Edition enlarged, with a familiar Method teaching how to cypher and decypher all private Transactions: Wherein are inserted the Keys by which the Lines of Text-writing affixed to those Cyphers are folded and unfolded. Invented and published by Mr. Noah Bridges. London, sold by Andrew Crook, 1662."

Bound up with some copies of Bridges's "Stenographie and Crytographie" is a work entitled: "Rarities: or, The incomparable Curiosities in Secret Writing, Both *aswel* by Waters *as* Cyphers, explained and made familiar to the meanest Capacity. *By which* Ministers of State may manage the Intrigues of Court and grand Concerns of Princes, the Ladies communicate their Amours, and every ordinary person (onely capable of legible Writing) may order his private affairs with all imaginable safety and secrecy. *Publish'd to promote the Publick, to dslight the Ingenious, and encourage the Industrious, By* G. B. *Gent. London*: Printed by *J. G.* for *Nath. Brook*, at the Angel in Cornhill. 1665." The contents consist of an address "To the Reader" signed "Thy more useful Friend G. B.", followed by 20 pages of text and a leaf (not numbered) containing a list of books sold by Nath. Brook. There is no indication as to the full name of G. B., who writes: "I think it fit to acquaint thee that several Cyphers and other Papers of Secret Writing which were many years since plunder'd from the Author of the following Tracts, came shortly after to my hands, and have lain long by me to little purpose; for notwithstanding his Publication of the following Discourse thereof, my great pains to make some progress therein came to nothing untill he in his second Edition gave the Learner Directions how to proceed: Since then I have made out his methods, and thereby understand his ingenious Contrivements of the Alphabets, and how he thereby Cyphers and Decyphers secret Concernments...." Copies of "Rarities" are in U.L.C. (L.32.59¹); B.L.O. (25788.f.22, wanting title-page); C.C.O. ("Ex dono Revd. Joshua Reynolds, S.T.B.", W.K.8.12); C.L.M. (Byrom coll., with inscription "A prsent from yᵉ Ingenious Author. October yᵉ 8.68. Samuel Cromleholme"); and W.J.C.

Bridges's shorthand follows in its main lines those of his predecessors, and includes an excessive number of arbitrary symbols, but his alphabet differs from them in some material respects. Initial and final vowels are expressed by a dot or "tittle" in various positions in relation to the consonantal character immediately following or preceding. Nearly all his precursors provided alphabetic symbols for the initial vowels. Although Lewis (*History of Shorthand*, 1816, p. 75) credits him with being the first to express the vowels regularly by dots, he was anticipated by Folkingham (see p. 27) and, according to Coles, by Walker. Bridges states that he received his rule for initial vowels from William Milburne of Putney, "a very ingenious youth, who I conceive invented the same". A William Milborne was church-warden at Putney in 1650.

NOAH BRIDGES (1610?–1672) was educated at Balliol College, Oxford, and acted as Clerk of the Parliament which sat in that city in 1643 and 1644. In 1645 Thomas Swadlin dedicated to him "The Souldiers Catechisme, composed for the Kings Armie", written at Bridges's suggestion in reply to Robert Ram's "Souldiers Catechisme, composed for the Parliaments Army". Bridges was created B.C.L. on 17 June 1646, being then "esteemed a most faithful subject to His Majesty". He was in attendance on Charles I in most of his restraints, especially at Newcastle and in the Isle of Wight. In return for his services the King granted him the office of Clerk of the House of Commons, but the appointment failed to pass the Great Seal because of the surrender of Oxford.

Bridges kept a private school at Putney for several years, among the subjects taught there in 1653 being "the Greek and Latin Tongues; also Arts and Sciences Mathematicall, viz. Arithmetique, Fair Writing, Merchants' Accounts, Geometry, Trigonometrie, Algebra, &c." Japhet, son of Noah Bridges by Katharine, was baptised at Putney on 4 December 1647, and a "chrisome child" of his was buried there on 13 March 1651/2. After the Restoration he vainly endeavoured to obtain the post of Clerk of the House of Commons, with survivorship to his son Japhet, who died in 1661. He also petitioned for the offices of comptroller, teller and weigher of the Mint, which the King had promised him, and of Gentleman Porter in the Tower.

Bridges was the author of "Vulgar Arithmetique, explayning the secrets of that Art, after a more exact and easie way than ever", London, 1653, and of "Lux Mercatoria, Arithmetick Natural and Decimal", London, 1661. His portrait by Faithorne, prefixed to "Vulgar Arithmetique", was re-engraved as Milton for Duroveray's edition of "Paradise Lost". The portrait by Loggan prefixed to his shorthand treatise also served as a frontispiece to "Lux Mercatoria". In his address to the reader of "Stenographie and Crytographie" he remarks that "a hand as long as thine arme is most fit to take the dreaming nonsence of our modern fanatiques".

The parish register of Putney records the burial of "Noah Bridges, esq.", on 19 June 1672. He is noticed in the *D.N.B.*

A Pen | Pluck'd from an | Eagles VVing. | Or, | The most Swift, Compendious, | and Speedy Method of | Short-Writing | That ever was yet Composed by any | in this Kingdom; | Is at length (through the blessing of God) | brought to Perfection, by the indefa- | tigable Industry of | William Mason, | Authour and Teacher of the said | Art. | *Omne bonum Dei donum.* | *Licensed and entred according to Order.* | *London*, Printed by *J. Darby*, for the Author. | Anno 1672.
[860¹.]

$6\frac{1}{2} \times 3\frac{7}{8}$ in., pp. (4) 71 letterpress, with headlines in B.L. Title within double-rule border. Sign. A–A8, B–I2 in fours. Shorthand characters inserted in MS.

Leaf 1ª Title, 1ᵇ blank, 2ª–2ᵇ To the Reader...Oct. 26. 71, followed by an acrostic signed G. N., 3ª–16ᵇ Text, 17ª–26ᵇ The practical table, 27ª–27ᵇ Six rules of directions, 28ª–38ª Index, 38ᵇ blank.

This is the first edition of Mason's first shorthand work. It was entered on the Stationers' Register to John Darby on 24 February 1671/2 (Roxb. *Transcript*, II, 440), and was announced in the "Term Catalogue", Easter 1672, as follows: "A pen pluckt from an Eagles Wing, or The most swift, compendious, and speedy, Method of Short-writing that was ever yet Composed. The Author, Will Mason, Teacher of the said Art in *Talbot Court*, in *Gracechurch street*. Printed for the Author; and sold by Brabazon Aylmer at the Three Pigeons in Cornhill, at 5s. bound, by reason the Characters are all writ with a Pen" (*T.C.* I, 105).

Other copies are in B.M.L. (787.a.73); B.L.O. (302.g.138); R.L.M. (Bailey coll., 514.H.68); C.L.W. (wanting title-page); B.G.P. (Guénin coll., Δ68166, wanting title-page); L.N.Y. (*KC(1672)); and W.J.C.

A so-called second edition was entitled "A Pen | Pluck'd From an | Eagles Wing. | Or | The Most Swift, Compendious, and Speedy Method of | Short-Writing. | The *Second Edition*, | With Additions, and Amendments. | *By* William Mason. | Writing-Master at the *Hand* and *Pen*, in | *Bell-Yard*, in *Grace-Church-Street*. | London | Printed for and Sold by the Author: Also by | *Chr. Coningsby*, at the *Golden Turks-Head*, | against St. *Dunstanes* Church, in *Fleet-street*, | *John Back*, at the *Black-Boy* on *London-* | *Bridge*. And other *Booksellers* in *London* and | *Westminster*. 1695." This is a reissue of the first edition with a new title-page, the contents and collation agreeing with the first. It was announced in the Term Catalogue, Trinity 1695 (*T.C.* II, 562). Copies of the "second edition" are in N.L.S. (Warden coll., Wn.837); L.N.Y. (Howard coll., Reserve); and W.J.C. A copy was in C.L.W.

Arts | Advancement | *or* | *The most Exact, Lineal,* | *Swift, Short, and* *Easy Method* | *of* | *Short-hand-Writing* | *hitherto Extent,* | *Is now (after* *a view of all others,* | *and above Twenty years Practice)* | *Built on a New* *Foundation, &* | *Raised to a higher degree of Per=* | *=fection than was* *ever before* | *Attained to by any.* | *Invented & Composed* | By | William Mason | *Teacher of the Art, in* | *Princes Court in Loathbury,* | *neare the Royal Exchange;* | London. | *Where these Books are to be had,* *&* | *such as desire to Learn may (by him)* | *be Expediciously Taught, at* | *Very Resonable Rates.* | *The Booke is also Sold by* | *these Book-sellers.* | *M͏ͬ Benj: Alsop at the Angel &* | *Bible, in the Poultry.* | *M͏ͬ Wilkins* *at ẙ Starr in Cheap side.* | *M͏ͬ Jacob Sampson just w:ᵗʰin Ludgate.* | *M͏ͬ Thom: Fox in Westminster Hall.* | *And severall others.* | *Price* *Bound, ı͏ˢ 6͏ᵈ* | *Printed for the Author.*1682 | *Ben: Rhodes sculpsit.*
[402⁹.]

$5\frac{5}{8} \times 2\frac{7}{8}$ in., 24 engraved plates (numbered 1–24), consisting of frontispiece portrait of Mason in oval with six lines below signed "S. W.", pictorial title-page, dedication to Sir Robert Clayton, Lord Mayor of London (plate 3), text (plates 4–6), table of words and sentences (plates 7–16), terminative rules, examples, contrarieties, specimen, etc. (plates 17–24), printed on one side.

This is the first edition of Mason's second shorthand work. It was advertised in the Term Catalogue, Hilary 1682, as follows: "There is newly published a very ingenious and highly approved piece of Short-Hand, curiously engraven on Copper, Intituled, Arts Advancement. Being the most Exact, Lineal, Swift, Short, and Easie, Method of Short-Hand Writing hitherto extant.... Invented and Composed by William Mason, Teacher of the Art, in Prince's Court, in Loathbury, near the Royal Exchange, London;...taught with great Expedition, and little Trouble to the Learner: the Author having contrived a very effectual way for Speed and Perfectness, and teaches the said Art at very reasonable Rates. The Book is also sold by several Booksellers in London and Westminster. Price, bound 1s. 6d." (*T.C.* 1, 481).

There are copies of this edition in B.M.L. (1043.b.52 and 1042.c.41, the latter wanting the frontispiece); B.L.O. (302.g.146); G.L.L. (C.8.4);

79

C.L.M. (Harland coll., Mun.D1.71, wanting port.); R.L.M. (Bailey coll., 514.H.69); N.L.S. (Warden coll., Wn.838); I.S.W.; L.N.Y. (Rockwell coll., *IDE); B.G.P. (Guénin coll., Δ68165¹); B.L.M.; and W.J.C.

Another issue of the 1682 edition has the name "Mʳ Ben: Harris under yᵉ: Royall Exch:" in place of "Mʳ Jacob Sampson just w:ᵗʰin Ludgate" on the title-page. Copies are in P.L.L. and W.J.C.

A later edition of "Arts Advancement", dated 1687, was called "*The Third Edition, Corrected and Enlarged* By William Mason *Author & Teacher of the said Art at his Writing School The Hand and Pen in* Bell-yard *Grace-Church Street* London", and was announced in the Term Catalogue, Hilary 1688 (*T.C.* ii, 220): Copies of the 1687 edition are in L.N.Y. (Beale coll., Reserve); the Heffley collection, Brooklyn, N.Y.; and W.J.C.

Another "*Third Edition, Corrected and Enlarged,* By William Mason, Author & Teacher of ÿ said Art, *At the Writing School, The Hand & Pen in* Scalding Alley *over against the Stocks-Market*" is dated 1699. Copies of this edition are in B.M.L. (G.16758.(6)); C.L.E. (Pocknell coll., 350R/653); N.L.S. (Warden coll., Wn.839); L.C.W. (Z56.M4); L.N.Y. (Beale coll., Reserve); and W.J.C.

An undated "Third Edition, Corrected and Enlarged" was published about 1719 with the imprint: "London *Printed for and Sold by* Ioseph Marshall *at the Bible in Newgate street* prⁱᶜᵉ *one Shilling, Likewise his*—1. La Plume Volante Prᵉ 2. ŝ. 2. Collection of Aphorisms pr. í. 3. Aurea Clavis or a Golden Key pr. 1s. 4. An easie table of Contractions pr. 6d. All Sold by Severall Booksellers. Copies are in P.L.L. (1682 added in MS.); N.L.S. (Warden coll.); B.G.P. (Guénin coll., Δ68165², Réserve); L.N.Y. (Howard coll., *KC (1720)); and W.J.C.

Mason's next publication appears to have been a large engraved sheet, 14 × 12 in., entitled "A Regular and Easie Table of Natural Contractions by the Persons, Moods, and Tenses; Each Character made from the Alphabet, & Vowels Places. The like never done by any other Hand. Composed by W:ᵐ Mason Writing Mʳ at the Hand and Pen in Bell-Yard between Grace

Church Street and Cornhill London. Harris Sculp." The sheet is undated, but is referred to in the Term Catalogue, Trinity 1695, as "his new sheet of Contractions by the Persons, Moods, and Tenses, etc." (*T.C.* II, 562), and is advertised in "Aurea Clavis", 1695 (see below). A copy is in B.M.L. (463.h.11 (4)), the last item in a volume of "Various Alphabets, Characters and Inscriptions collected by Joseph Ames". Mason's address and the engraver's name are omitted from later issues of the "Table".

A key to the above was published in the same year, with the following title: "Aurea Clavis: or, a Golden Key to the Cabinet of Contractions: Unlocking all the Misteries (and seeming Difficulties) of an Engraven Sheet of Short-Hand Lately Published, Entituled, *A Regular and Easy Table of Natural Contractions by the Persons, Moods, and Tenses*, &c. By *William Mason*, Writing-Master, at the *Hand* and *Pen* in *Bell-Yard*, between *Grace-Church-Street* and *Cornhill, London*. It being nearly suited to His Late *Short-Hand-Book*, Entituled, *Arts Advancement*, &c. But more Exactly Adapted to a *Short-Hand*, in *Manuscript*, which he now Teacheth. This present Clavis is suited to the Meanest Capacity, and gives Directions how to Apply the said *Contractions* to any other *Short-Hand*: Instance being given at the End of this Book. *London*, Printed for, and Sold by, the *Author* above-said: Also by *C. Coningsby*, at the *Golden Turks Head*, against St. *Dunstan*'s Church, in *Fleet-street*. *R. Cumberland*, at the *Angel* in St. *Paul*'s Church-yard. *J. Back*, at the *Black-Boy* on *London-Bridge*; and other *Booksellers* in *London* and *Westminster*, 1695." Copies of this first edition (referred to in the Term Catalogue, Trinity 1695 (*T.C.* II, 562)) are in Dr Williams's Library, Gordon Square, London, and W.J.C.

Another edition of "Aurea Clavis" is described on the title-page as "By William Mason: and now taught by Joseph Smith Writing Master (one of his pupils) at the Hand and Pen in the Poultry, near the Church". The imprint of this edition reads: "London, Printed for the Author: and Sold by Joseph Marshall, at the Bible in Newgate-street; D. Brown, without Temple-bar; at Mercers-Chapel in Cheapside; N. Crouch in the Poultrey; Andrew Bell in Cornhill; T. Harrison, at the corner of the Royal Exchange; J. Marshall in Gracechurch-street; and E. Tracy on London-Bridge. 1719." Copies are in B.M.L. (7942.a.36.(2)) and P.L.L.

In 1707 Mason published a third system of shorthand, entitled "*La Plume Volante*, or, the Art of Short-Hand Improv'd. Being the most Swift, Regular, and Easy Method of *Short-Hand-Writing* yet Extant. Compos'd after Forty Years Practice and Improvement of the said Art, by the Observation of other Methods, and the Intent Study of it, by William Mason. *London*: Printed for the Author, at the *Hand* and *Pen* in the *Poultrey*, near the Church: Where the Books are to be had, and such as please may be Expeditiously Taught, on Reasonable Terms. It is also Sold by these Booksellers following; *Viz.* Mr. *D. Brown*, at the *Black Swan* without *Temple-Bar*. *J. Baker*, at *Mercers Chappel* in *Cheap-side*. *Andrew Bell*, at the *Cross Keys* in *Cornhil*, and *John Marshall*, in *Grace-Church-street*. 1707. Price 2*s*." In this system, which Mason claimed to have taught in manuscript for fifteen years previously, only five of Rich's characters were retained, and many improvements were introduced. It was announced in the Term Catalogue, Trinity 1707 (*T.C.* III, 559). Copies of the first edition of 1707 are in the B.M.L. (1042.b.46); L.P.L. (105.B.8); B.L.O. (302.g.143); R.L.M. (Bailey coll., 514.H.70); C.L.M. (Byrom coll., 2.I.1.67); N.L.S. (Warden coll., Wn.841); S.L.D. (C.a.13); L.N.Y. (Beale coll., *IDE); and W.J.C.

Another edition of "La Plume Volante" was published in 1719 with the following imprint: "*London*, Taught by *Jos. Smith*, at the *Hand & Pen* in the *Poultry*, near the *Church*; where the Books are to be had. Also Sold by *Joseph Marshall*, at the Bible in *Newgate-Street*, D. Browne without Temple-Bar, at Mercers-Chappel in Cheapside, N. Crowch in the Poultry, A. Bell at the Cross-Keys in Cornhill, T. Harrison, the Corner of the Royal-Exchange, J. Marshall in Gracechurch-Street, and by Tracey on *London-Bridge*, 1719. price 2s." Copies of this edition are in P.L.L.; N.L.S. (Warden coll., Wn.842); S.L.D. (C.a.13); P.L.S. (Paterson coll.); and W.J.C.

An undated "Fifth Edition, with the Addition of the Terms of the Law, and much Amended" carries the imprint: "*London*, Taught by *Jos Smith*, at the *Hand* and *Pen* in the *Poultry*, near the *Church*; where the Books are to be had. Also Printed and Sold by *Joseph Marshal*, at the Bible in *Newgate-Street*. *D Browne*, without Temple-Bar. *J. Marshal*, in Gracechurch-

Street. Price 2*s*. 6*d*." This is probably a posthumous edition, issued about 1728. The statement on the title-page is amended to read: "Compos'd after Fifty Years Practice", etc. A crude woodcut portrait of Mason is prefixed, with four lines of verse below. The text is preceded by a list of six books "newly printed for and sold by" Marshall, and five more are listed on the last page. Copies of this edition are in P.L.L.; N.L.S. (Warden coll., Wn.843); B.N.P. (V.25060); L.N.Y. (Beale coll., *IDS p.v.274, no. 1, and *IDE); and W.J.C.

Another undated "Fifth Edition" has the imprint: "*London*, Taught by *Jos Smith*, at the *Hand* and *Pen* in the *Poultry*, near the *Church*; where the Books are to be had. Also Printed and Sold by *Joseph Marshal*, at the Bible in *Newgate-Street*. Price 2*s*. 6*d*. Where may be had all D. *Owen's*, Works *Bunyan's* and *Keaches*, Works." In this edition the list of books advertised preceding the text is extended from six to twelve. Copies are in B.M.L. (1042.b.47 and 7942.a.11); G.L.L. (C.8.4); R.L.M. (Bailey coll., 514.H.70); C.L.M. (Harland coll., Mun.D1.74); P.L.L.; N.L.S. (Warden coll., Wn.844); L.C.W.; L.N.Y.; U.L.Y.; and W.J.C. Some copies of this edition (B.M.1042.b.47, G.L.L. and R.L.M.) have the engraved sheet "A Regular and Easie Table of Natural Contractions", etc., inserted. Some copies (W.J.C.) have twelve additional pages at the end containing a long list of "Books Printed for and sold by Joseph Marshall, Senior and Junior, at the Bible in Newgate-Street, over-against the Blue-Court-Gate." As one of the books in this list was printed in 1734, the copies containing it must have been issued later than 1733.

Another undated edition is called "The Fifth Edition. *With the Addition of the Terms of the Law, and much Amended; and a regular and easy Table of Contractions, by the Persons, Moods and Tenses on a large Copper-Plate. By* William Mason. *London:* Printed for George Keith, at the *Bible* and *Crown*, in *Gracechurch-Street*. [Price 2*s*. 6*d*. Bound.]" It contains the list of twelve books printed for Marshall, and the further list of five books on the last page, as well as the folding engraved plate announced on the title-page, from which Mason's address has been deleted. Copies of this edition are in the G.L.L. (C.8.4); I.S.W.; R.L.M. (Bailey coll., 514.H.71); C.L.E. (Pocknell coll., 351R/653); N.L.S. (Warden coll., Wn.845); C.L.W.;

B.G.P. (Guénin coll., Δ68167); L.N.Y. (Beale coll., *IDS p.v.274, no. 2); and W.J.C.

The last shorthand book issued by William Mason was entitled "*Mason's Short-Hand Exemplify'd: in a Collection of Aphorisms, and Reflections Moral and Political. Design'd for the Easy and Speedy Improvement of Practitioners in the said Art. By W. Mason, at his Writing-School, in Token-House-Yard, in Leaden-Hall-Street, near the Market, London. London, Printed by B. Mills, for the Author, and sold by the Booksellers of London and Westminster.* 1712." Two copies only are recorded, both in W.J.C. One of these has a slip of errata pasted on the verso of the title, and the date has been altered in MS. to 1714.

Apart from the Bible, New Testament and Psalms, "Mason's Short-Hand Exemplify'd" is the earliest known separate publication designed to serve as a reading or exercise book in shorthand.

William Mason was the author of three different systems of shorthand. The first ("A Pen pluck'd from an Eagles Wing", 1672) was, as he said, "chiefly founded on Mr. Rich's scheme", nearly all Rich's alphabetic characters being retained. Mason, however, provided alternative signs for *p* and reverted to the five-vowel scale of Shelton.

In "Arts Advancement" (1682) he discarded all but six of Rich's characters and took a great stride forward by reducing the vowel places to three, *a* and *e* being allotted a position at the head, *i* in the middle, *o* and *u* at the foot of the consonantal character. The sacrifice of phonetic precision which this entailed was offset by greater fluency of writing, the necessity of placing a succeeding consonant immediately above or below its predecessor being obviated. To minimise the risk of confusion, the author counselled the writing of *e* and *u* at a slightly greater distance from the consonant than *a* and *o*, a nice distinction which must have been difficult to observe in practice. Initial vowels were expressed by their alphabetic symbols and final vowels by a dot in the allotted position. In this system Mason assigned the same character to *c* and *k*. The sounds of *b* and *p* being "very near alike", he represented *b* by a long horizontal curve, *p* by a shorter one. Similarly, he recognised the phonetic

84

affinity between *s* and *z* by making the diagonal / serve for both, while recommending the learner to write it "longer and stronger" for *z*. This seems to have been the first tentative essay at pairing related consonants by thickening, a prominent feature of Pitman's and many later systems. An alternative sign for *s* was the circle which Farthing had already introduced for the same purpose, but whilst Farthing used the circle initially, medially and finally, Mason restricted its employment to effect the junction between two other consonants. An ingenious abbreviating rule was versified thus:

"Such word or words as in a sentence ends
With the same letter the next word begins,
That letter (so repeated) single write,
And several words in one you will unite."

In his table of "natural contractions" Mason attempted to show the persons, moods and tenses by the position in which they were written, before or after the pronoun.

The alphabet was further simplified in Mason's third system ("La Plume Volante", 1707), and alternative signs were provided for *b*, *q*, *s*, *u* and *x*. The learner was recommended to "omit silent letters and enlarge emphatical ones". In accordance with this rule the *m* in the word "empty" was written larger than the *t*, the *p* being of course omitted.

Mason's third system was republished in 1750 by Thomas Gurney, with slight modifications, and thus given a new lease of life which has extended to the present day, although the number of practitioners of the system must now be very small indeed.

WILLIAM MASON (1645?–1718?), a London writing master, has been called "the most celebrated shorthand writer of the 17th century" (J. H. Lewis's *Historical Account of the Rise and Progress of Shorthand*, 1816, p. 76) and "an inventor who stands head and shoulders above his fellows of the same epoch" (H. W. Innes and G. C. Mares, "Critical and Historical Account of the Art of Shorthand", in *The National Stenographer*, 1892, p. 171). Some of the improvements with which he has been credited, however, had been adopted by his predecessors. He told the readers of "La Plume Volante" (1707) that he had

85

delighted in the art of shorthand from his youth, and had practised various methods before attempting to compose one of his own. As the title-page of "Arts Advancement" (1687) refers to twenty-eight years' practice of stenography, his shorthand studies must have begun at least as early as 1659. The preface to his first book is dated 26 October 1671 "from my Study in Lothbury", and at Easter 1672 he was giving lessons in Talbot Court, Gracechurch Street, but it is clear that he had been teaching the art for some years previously.

William Mason was one of those who recommended to the public the first edition of Cocker's "Arithmetick" in 1678. Four years later when he published his "Arts Advancement" with a dedication to Sir Robert Clayton, he was teaching this new system in Princes Court, Lothbury, near the Royal Exchange. In 1687 he had established a writing school at the Hand and Pen in Bell Yard, between Gracechurch Street and Cornhill, where he seems to have remained for a decade or so, though he offered to attend pupils "at their own habitations". By 1699 he had removed to the Hand and Pen in Scalding Alley, opposite the Stocks Market (afterwards renamed St Mildred's Court), this being the address given by Pepys in his "Alphabetical List of surviving Maister-Pen-Men"; but in 1707 he is found at the Hand and Pen in the Poultry, near the church.

Mason's writing school was located in 1712 in Tokenhouse Yard, Leadenhall Street, near the Market, and four years later he was living next door to Leadenhall Coffee-House in Leadenhall Street, where he gave instruction in shorthand twice weekly and had a room set apart for the purpose which he called "the Stenographical Club Room" (*Monthly Catalogue*, November 1716). He advertised extensively in the news sheets of the time, and his school appears to have been well patronised. One of his pupils, Joseph Smith, succeeded him at the Hand and Pen in the Poultry about 1719 and taught his shorthand there, a fact which seems to point to Mason's having died or retired shortly before.

On the last page of the first edition of "Arts Advancement" Mason had announced that "If the Lord continues Life and Health to ye Author of this Book, & it finds acceptance with the World, he will be encouraged to prosecute his designes of Ingraving and Printing the whole Bible in the same Character: A thing never yet done by any." This statement was modified in the 1687 edition, Addy's shorthand Bible having appeared in the meantime (see p. 105), and the last seven words were replaced by: "If not a large Alphabetical Dictionary." ·Neither Bible nor dictionary is known to have been published.

In addition to his reputation as a shorthand author and teacher, Mason was, according to a contemporary writer, "very famous in writing many things in a little compass" (William Turner's *Compleat History of the most Remarkable Providences...in this Present Age,* 1697, pt. iii, p. 26). One such exploit is noticed in Bagford's MS. Catalogue of Copy Books as follows: "Wm Mason of Cannon Street graved in ye Compass of an Heart ye number of Letters, words, Chapters and verses in ye Bible." In the historical introduction to Joseph Champion's "The Parallel; or, Comparative Penmanship Exemplified", 1749, Mason's name is mentioned in company with others who were famous for writing in miniature. Mr Alexander Paterson's statement that Mason was "a classical scholar and the author of a Hebrew Grammar" (*Phonetic Journal,* 1899, p. 742) appears to be based on a misapprehension. Among the books sold by him and advertised at the end of "Aurea Clavis" was "A Comprehensive Grammar, containing the most Material and Necessary Rules for the Reading and Attaining the Hebrew Tongue"; but the author of this grammar was Jehudah Stennett, and whatever the stenographer's classical attainments may have been, there is no evidence that they extended to a knowledge of Hebrew.

(*D.N.B.*; Sir Ambrose Heal's *The English Writing-Masters and their Copy-Books,* 1931, p. 73; *Phonetic Journal,* XLV, 201–2, 24 April 1886; *ibid.* LVIII, 742, 25 Nov. 1899.)

The | Newest, Plainest, | and the Shortest | Short-hand, | containing| 1. A brief account of all the Short-hands | already Extant; with their Alphabets, | and fundamental rules. | 2. A plain and easie Method for begin- | ners, less burthensome to the memory | than any other. | 3. A new invention for contracting words, | with special rules for contracting sen- | tences, and other ingenious fancies both | pleasant and profitable unto all, let their | Character be whose or what it will. | By *E. Coles,* School-master in *Russel-* | *street,* by *Covent-Garden.* | *London,* Printed for *Peter Parker,* at the sign of | the *Leg* and *Star;* over against the *Royal* | *Exchange,* in *Cornhil,* 1674.
[860 5.]

$6\frac{3}{4} \times 4\frac{1}{4}$ in., 8vo, pp. (2) + 27 letterpress, and 7 double-page engraved plates (numbered 1 to 7) printed on one side. With headlines. Sign. A–B7 in eights.

Leaf 1ª Title, 1ᵇ blank, 2ª–2ᵇ Authors of short-hand, &c., 3ª blank, 3ᵇ List of 14 shorthand alphabets, 4ª Synopses of alphabets, 4ᵇ blank, 5ª Observations on earlier systems, 5ᵇ–7ª Two general rules, 7ᵇ–8ª blank, 8ᵇ Alphabet, words, etc., 9ª Rules for syllables, 9ᵇ–10ª blank, 10ᵇ–11ª The Table of Prepositions & Terminations, 11ᵇ–12ª blank, 12ᵇ–13ª Six Additional Terminative Rules, 13ᵇ–14ª blank, 14ᵇ Adjectives, 15ª A very short and easie Table of our most usuall words, 15ᵇ–16ª blank, 16ᵇ Table of usual words continued, 17ª The Bible books contracted, 17ᵇ blank, 18ª–22ᵇ A regular Improvement, etc., 23ª blank, 23ᵇ–24ª The Table of Symbolicalls, 24ᵇ blank, 25ª–29ª Explanation of the symbolicals, 29ᵇ blank.

This is doubtless the first edition. It was announced in the Term Catalogue, Easter 1674, "Price, stitcht, 1s." (*T.C.* 1, 172). There are copies in B.L.O. (8° P.148.Art); U.L.C. (Dd.*4.56²(F)); L.C.W. (Z56.C69); L.N.Y. (Beale coll., *IDS p.v.12, no. 8); Watkinson Library, Hartford, Conn., U.S.A. (Blair coll.); J.R.G.; and W.J.C.

No copy of any edition between the first and the tenth is recorded. The tenth edition is entitled "The newest, plainest and best shorthand extant.... By E. Coles, late school-master in Russell-street, by Covent-garden. London, printed for John Marshall, at the Bible in Gracechurch-street. 1707." To this is prefixed an engraved portrait of Coles in wig and bands, which is of doubtful authenticity. It was announced in the Term Catalogue, Hilary 1707, price 1s. (*T.C.* III, 538). Copies of this edition are in B.M.L. (12991.ccc.18); U.L.C. (L.32.51³); L.N.Y. (Howard coll., Reserve, incomplete); S.L.D. (C.a.12, wanting portrait); Royal Library, Copenhagen; J.R.G.; and W.J.C.

Coles's book is noteworthy for two reasons. It contains the first attempt at a historical account of shorthand systems, and it introduces the important principle of vowel indication by varying the position of the consonants in relation to the line of writing. The author points out that the shortest words present the greatest obstacles in writing shorthand and that the English language consists largely of monosyllables, to which he paid special attention. "Every syllable", he says, "should be answer'd by a single dash and every word of one syllable by once setting of the pen to paper." He accordingly provides for the implication of the vowels in monosyllables by writing the initial consonant above, on or below a real or imaginary line, and suggests that the same principle may be applied to other words. Coles rejected as ambiguous the rules laid down by Rich and Everardt for contracting sentences, judiciously observing that many of them are "so frivolous, or tedious, that one had better write them out at length".

ELISHA COLES (1640?–1680?), author of "The Newest, Plainest and the Shortest Short-Hand", is identified by Thompson Cooper in the *D.N.B.* with Elisha, son of John Coles (1623?–1678), schoolmaster at Wolverhampton, and nephew of Elisha Coles (1608?–1688), the Calvinistic author of "A Practical Discourse of God's Sovereignty", 1673. Gerald Mander, on the other hand, considers that he was probably the son of Elisha Coles, the Calvinist (*The Identity of Elisha Coles*, 1919).

In "The Compleat English Schoolmaster", 1674, of which the stenographer acknowledged the paternity (*Short-Hand*, 1674, p. 6), Coles writes: "I was born and bred [for a dozen years] in the very heart of England, I spent almost as many in her very eye,[1] and after that as many more in [or about] the very head of all the Kingdom." This would give a date near 1640 for Coles's birth, as suggested by the *D.N.B.*, and is consistent with Wood's statement that Northamptonshire was his native county. Wood adds that he "entered into Magdalen College in the latter part of 1658, left it without taking of a degree, retired to London, taught Latin there to youths, and English to foreigners about 1663. Afterwards he continued that employment with good success in Russell-street near Covent Garden, within the liberty of Westminster, and at length became one of the ushers of Merchant-Taylors' School; but upon some default, not now to be named, he left all, and went into Ireland where he ended his course" (*Ath. Oxon.* ed. Bliss, III, 1274).

An Elisha Coles was chorister of Magdalen College, Oxford (1658–1661), and on 26 March 1659 matriculated as a "plebian" of that university (Bloxham's *Reg. Magd. Coll.* 1853, p. 81), which he left without taking a degree. John

---

[1] I.e. Oxford. See *Notes and Queries*, CLXV, 49 (22 July 1933).

Coles had been appointed First Undermaster at Merchant Taylors' School in 1652, and an Elisha Coles was entered on the admission register of the school on 11 March 1663/4. In February 1677 he "was a Suitor to be School Master of Wolverhampton School in the roome of his late Father decd." In this he was unsuccessful, but was given the humbler post of Second Undermaster at Merchant Taylors' School on 3 August 1677. On 14 December 1678, writing from Dublin, he resigned his position in London, having "without any seeking" obtained a better one. This was the mastership of the Free School founded by Erasmus Smith at Galway, where he is said to have died on 20 December 1680 (Hardiman's *History of Galway*, 1820, p. 252). The epitaph on his gravestone in the south aisle of St Nicholas's Church described him as "Master of Arts and of the Languages".

Coles has been credited with the authorship of about ten different works, but it is possible that not all of them were from the same pen. "Χριστολογία, or a Metrical Paraphrase on the History of our Lord and Saviour Jesus Christ", 1671, is ascribed by Wood to Elisha, son of Elisha Coles the Calvinist, but on the title-page of the 1680 edition the author is given as "Elisha Coles, late of Magd. Coll. Oxon." It is an extraordinary achievement, running to more than a hundred pages, each page containing forty-four lines of verse. The address to the reader is signed "Elisha Coles, Junior". The following publications may be attributed with some confidence to the stenographer:

1. "The Compleat English Schoolmaster. Or the Most Natural and Easie Method of Spelling English. According to the present proper pronuntiation of the Language in Oxford and London. Wherein Children and Foreigners shall have the whole Body of English words in the plainest order digested and divided to their hands. To which is added an Appendix of useful Observations on Orthography. . . . London, Printed for Peter Parker, at the sign of the Leg and Star, over against the Royal Exchange, in Cornhil, 1674." ("To the Reader" signed "C. Coles".) B.L.O.

2. "Nolens Volens: or, you shall make Latin, whether you will or no. Containing the plainest Directions that have yet been given on that subject. Together with the Youths Visible Bible. . . London: Printed by Andrew Clark for T. Basset, at the Church in Fleet Street, and H. Brome, at the Gun at the West End of S. Pauls. 1675." The address to the reader concludes: "These observations will assist you much, in the giving of apposite English to your

Latin; which is a thing of greater moment than many apprehend. And therefore I intend a more Particular Discourse upon that Subject, if God grant Life and Opportunity to Your Friend and Servant Elisha Coles." This promise was fulfilled by the publication of

3. "Syncrisis, or the Most Natural and Easie Method of Learning Latin: by Comparing it with English Together with the Holy History of Scripture-War. . . . London, Printed by H. L. for Tho. Drant at the Ship in St. Mary Axe, and Tho. Lacey at the Golden Lion, near the Meal-Market Southwark. 1675." The preface is signed "E. Coles", and in dedicating his book "to the Reverend Company of Authorised School-masters, both Publick and Private", he claims to have followed the principle of syncrisis, or comparison of one language with another, "in Learning above twenty years, and in teaching Latin about fourteen, though tis but of late that I am encouraged to Publish my Essays (in various Methods) for improving of it". At the end of the introduction, part 1, Coles writes: "A larger Account of all our Abbreviations you'll have at the end of my Spelling Book, Printed for Peter Parker."

4. "An English Dictionary. . . . By E. Coles, School-Master and Teacher of the Tongue to Forreigners. . . . London, Printed for Samuel Crouch, at the Corner Shop of Popes-head Ally, on the right hand next Cornhill. 1676." The books for sale by Peter Parker listed at the end include "The Compleat English School-master, . . . by Elisha Coles, School-master", and "The Newest, Plainest and Shortest Shorthand, . . . by Elisha Coles, School-master".

5. "A Dictionary, English-Latin, and Latin-English, Containing all things Necessary for the Translating of either Language into the other. . . . By Elisha Coles late of Magdalen Colledge, Oxon, now one of the Ushers in Merchant-Taylors School, London. Printed by John Richardson, for Peter Parker, at the Leg and Star over against the Royal-Exchange: And Thomas and John Guy, at the Corner Shop of Little Lumbard-street and Cornhill, 1677." (On A2^b is advertised "An English Dictionary, lately published by the same Author Mr. Elisha Coles".) The title-page of the 1679 edition omits the reference to Merchant Taylors' School, Coles having resigned in the previous year. Prefixed is Charles II's licence granting to the author the sole right of printing and publishing the book for fourteen years.

(*D.N.B.*; Sir Ambrose Heal's *The English Writing-Masters and their Copy-Books*, 1931, pp. 37–8; Gerald Mander's *The Identity of Elisha Coles*, 1919.)

Maximum | In | Minimo | or | Mr *Jeremiah Rich^s* | Pens Dexterity compleated | With the Whole terms of the law | by | *Samuel Botley* | London *Printed for* John Man | *at the heart and Bible in* | *Cornhill near the Royall* | *Exchange.* | *Where also The Psalmes &* | *the new Testament* | *Curiously Engraven* | *and Printed in the* | *same Character* | *are to be* | *sold.* [860^4.]

6$\frac{1}{2}$ × 4$\frac{1}{4}$ in., 8vo, 33 engraved leaves printed on one side. No numbers to pages. N.D. (1692?).

Leaf 1^a blank, 1^b Portrait of Rich, 2^a Portrait of Botley "Ano 1674 Ætat suæ 33", 2^b blank, 3^a Title within oval cartouche below the royal arms and the Lord's Prayer, the Creed and the Ten Commandments in minute shorthand characters, 3^b–4^a blank, 4^b Verses by E. G., 5^a Botley's address "To all my Scholars in London Bristoll and Exeter and the Intelligent Reader", 5^b–6^a blank, 6^b–7^a Text, 7^b–8^a blank, 8^b–9^a Text, 9^b–10^a blank, 10^b–11^a Text, 11^b–12^a blank, 12^b–13^a Text, 13^b–14^a blank, 14^b–15^a Text, 15^b–16^a blank, 16^b Text, 17^a–25^a Alphabetical list of examples, 25^b–26^a blank, 26^b–33^a The whole Terms of the Law in Mr Rich's Character, 33^b blank. The ten double-page plates of the text and list of examples are lettered A to K. The engraver's name, "Tho: Burnford", appears at the foot of leaf 5^a.

This is probably a posthumous edition of Botley's "Maximum in Minimo". John Man, the printer, was at the Heart and Bible in 1692. An earlier imprint at the foot of the title-page has been obliterated from the plate. The Pepysian copy, which is bound with other shorthand pamphlets in vol. 4 of the collection, has been trimmed by the binder to 6$\frac{1}{2}$ × 4 in.

Other copies are in U.L.C. (Bb*.12.21^2); L.N.Y. (Howard coll., *KC (169–)); P.L.S. (Paterson coll.); B.G.P. (Guénin coll., ∆67848^1); and W.J.C.

The first edition appears to have been published late in 1674 or early in 1675. It was entered on the Stationers' Register to Benjamin Foster on 30 November 1674 (Arber's *Transcript*, II, 492) and advertised in the Term Catalogue,

Hilary 1675, as "Printed by Samuel Botley, Teacher of the said Art, at his House in *Thames* street, over against Vintners Hall; with all the Terms of Law, in Latin, French, and English, in the same Book. Price, 2s. 6d. Where also the *Psalms* at 5s., and the *New Testament* at 10s., curiously bound and Printed in the same Character (which all Short-Hands that ever were, could never afford the like), are sold, by Robert Clavell at the Peacock in St. *Paul's* Church-yard, and John Leigh at the Bell in *Fleet street*" (*T.C.* 1, 201). The imprint at the foot of the title-page reads: "London *Printed and sould by* Samuel Botley *and no where else.*" This edition contains a dedication to "Mr. Thomas Bard of London Gent" and verses signed I. H. which are not found in subsequent editions. The portrait of Botley bears the name of the engraver, William Dolle, which does not appear on the re-engraved portrait prefixed to later editions. Copies are in B.M.L. (1042.c.29); P.L.L. (wanting the two portraits); U.L.C. (L.32.56¹); R.L.M. (Bailey coll., 514.G.1, wanting the last two leaves); N.L.S. (Warden coll., Wn.825); B.G.P. (Guénin coll., Δ67848²); L.N.Y. (Rockwell coll., *KC (1674), wanting last two leaves, and Heffley coll., *KC (1674)); and W.J.C.

A reprint was announced in the Term Catalogue, Trinity 1676: "Price 2s. 6d. Sold by Robert Clavell at the Peacock in St. *Paul's* Churchyard; where the *Psalms* and the *New Testament* curiously printed in the same Character are to be sold" (*T.C.* 1, 249).

Another reprint was announced in the Term Catalogue, Hilary 1677/8, with the New Testament and Psalms in shorthand, "bound up in gilt; all which are sold much cheaper than formerly by R. Clavell at the Peacock in St. Paul's Churchyard: and the said Art of Short-Writing is now taught by Mr. Brady on Dowgate Hill" (*T.C.* 1, 305). A copy with the imprint "London Printed and sould by Robert Clavell" was in the Howard collection.

An issue similar in every respect to that in the Pepysian Library, but with the name "Natʰ Sackett" substituted for that of John Man, and containing the re-engraved portraits of Rich and Botley, was published in or about 1698, when Sackett had succeeded Man at the Heart and Bible. Copies are in

B.M.L. (1043.b.64); R.L.M. (Bailey coll., 514.G.3); N.L.S. (Warden coll., Wn.826 and 53); G.L.L. (C.8.4); L.C.W. (Z56.B751); L.N.Y. (Beale coll., *KC (169–)); U.L.Y. (Healey coll., F25.340); and W.J.C.

Another edition bears the imprint: "London: *Printed for Edmund Parker at the Bible and Crown in Lambard street. price (1ˢ: 6ᵖ).*" Copies are in B.M.L. (1042.b.50); B.L.O. (302.g.137); R.L.M. (Bailey coll., 514.G.2); L.N.Y. (Howard coll., *KC (170–)); and W.J.C. Edmund Parker established himself at the above address in 1704.

A later edition has the imprint: "London: Printed for Edmund Parker at the *Bible* and *Crown* in *Lombard-Street* near *Stocks-Market*. (Price 1*s*. 6*d*.) Lately Publish'd, The London New Method and Art of Teaching Children to Spell and Read. *Price Bound 6d.*" Copies are in N.L.S. (Warden coll., Wn.52); C.L.M. (Mun.D.1.86); S.L.D.; and L.N.Y. (Howard coll., *KC (1711)). "The London New Method", etc., was advertised in *Mist's Journal*, 7 Nov. 1719.

As its title indicates, Botley's "Maximum in Minimo" embodied the system of Jeremiah Rich (see p. 62). It had few original features except the alphabetical list of law terms "never done before by any till now" and a pictorial indication of the price of the book by a crown halved vertically. The prices of the Psalms and of the New Testament are similarly shown on the last page by illustrations of a complete crown and an angel. A copy of Botley's work formerly owned by J. H. Lewis, the shorthand historian, bore the caustic comment on one of the end-papers: "To learn this book through your heed ought to be as large as St. Paul's Doom by God!"

SAMUEL BOTLEY (1641–1677) was the son of Robert Botley, citizen and cordwainer of London. He was admitted to the freedom of the Cordwainers' Company "by patrimony" on 12 April 1662, his brother Benjamin being admitted a year later. In 1668 he was Messenger of the Chamber in the Lord Chamberlain's Department, and on 3 May 1672 his name is found appended to a receipt for a licence granted under the Declaration of Indulgence in mitigation of the rigours of the Conventicle and Five-Mile Acts to Thomas Goldham to preach in his own house at Burwash, Sussex (*S.P.Dom. Car. II*, 320).

An advertisement in the Term Catalogue of 24 November 1673 (*T.C.* 1, 160) shows that Botley was then teaching shorthand "over against Vintners Hall in Thames-street", where he sold Rich's New Testament and Psalms as well as his engraved table (see pp. 56, 60, 61). Subsequently he was teaching at "Colonel Mason's Coffee house in Cornhill". He also had scholars at Bristol and Exeter, and in his address to them prefixed to "Maximum in Minimo" alludes to "my other various concerns impeding my constant personal attendance". On sheet K2 of his book he brackets his Christian name with that of his wife Hannah.

The register of St James Garlickhithe records that "Mr. Samuell Botley, Free of the Cordwainers, dyed of the stoppage of the stomach and was Buried in St. Thomas Apostles the 18th day of October 1677 out of Thames Street". His burial is also recorded in the register of St Thomas the Apostle. In the last-named register the burial of Mary, daughter of Samuel and Hannah Botley, is recorded on 4 November 1677.

(A. T. Wright's *Jeremiah Rich*, 1911, pp. 84–8.)

Rich Redivivus | or | *M*ʳ *Jeremiah Richs* | Short-Hand *ImProved* | *In a more Breife & Easy* | *Method then Hath* | *been Set forth by Any* | *here to fore, Now made* | *Publique for Generall* | *Advantage By* | *Nathaniell Stringer* | *A Quondam Scholar* | *To the said M*ʳ *Rich* | *Licensed by Roger Lestrange* | *London Printed and are to be sould by* | *Richard Northcott next S*ᵗ *Peeters* | *Alley in Cornhill and att the* | *Marriners and Anchor on fish street hill* | *The third edition ~ 1686* | *the price of the Booke 1*ˢ | *Iohannis Drapentier Sculp*   [1111².]

$7\frac{1}{8} \times 4\frac{5}{8}$ in., 8vo, 12 leaves engraved throughout on one side (including portrait and title-page). The title-page is elaborately engraved by John Drapentier (Johnson, No. 1), with the Lord's Prayer in minute shorthand characters in a circle at the top, followed by the date 1676. The side panels contain the Lord's Prayer, the Creed, "A Prayer for yᵉ Kings Maˢᵗy", the Ten Commandments and "A Prayer for yᵉ Royall family", all in shorthand. Between the title proper and the imprint are the arms of Stringer. No numbers to pages. No headlines. No signatures.

95

Leaf 1ᵃ blank, 1ᵇ Portrait of Stringer with 6 lines of verse below signed "H. C.", 2ᵃ Title page, 2ᵇ blank, 3ᵃ blank, 3ᵇ "To the Ingenious peruser... Nathaniell Stringer" and verses, 4ᵃ Verses by Hen: Care and I. W., 4ᵇ–5ᵃ blank, 5ᵇ–6ᵃ Text, 6ᵇ–7ᵃ blank, 7ᵇ–8ᵃ Text, 8ᵇ–9ᵃ blank, 9ᵇ–10ᵃ Text, 10ᵇ–11ᵃ blank, 11ᵇ–12ᵃ Text, 12ᵇ blank.

Copies of this edition are in U.L.C. (Adams 7.68.14); C.L.M. (Harland coll., Mun.D.1.86, wanting portrait); C.L.E. (Pocknell coll., 528R/653); N.L.S. (Blair and Warden colls., Wn.505); C.L.W. (Walford coll.); B.L.M.; and W.J.C.

The first edition of "Rich Redivivus" has the same title as in subsequent editions, but the imprint reads: "London Printed and are to be sould by Richard Northcott next Sᵗ Peeters Alley in Cornhill and att the Marriners and Anchor on fish street hill and by Ben: Haris, at yᵉ Stationers armes in sweetings Rents yᵉ East end of yᵉ Royall Exchange in Corn hil ~ the price of the Booke 1ˢ Iohannis Drapentier Sculp". It was announced in the Term Catalogue, Easter 1677, under "Miscellanies" (*T.C.* I, 275). The only copy located is in B.M.L. (1043.b.57).

No copy of the second edition is known to be extant.

A fourth edition was announced in the Term Catalogue, Trinity 1694, as "The Fourth Edition. Octavo. Price 1s. Printed for W. Marshall at the Bible in Newgate street" (*T.C.* II, 515). No copy with this imprint has been traced, but the announcement may refer to an edition with the following imprint: "London Printed for William Marshall at the Bible in Newgate Street, And John Marshall at the Bible in Gracious Street", of which copies are in U.L.C. (L.32.50³) and R.L.M. (Bailey coll., 514.L.1). This edition consists of fourteen engraved leaves printed on one side, the right-hand plates being numbered at the foot 2, 3, 4, 5, 6, Finis. The text on page 4 (right) is repeated on page 6 (left and right).

Another edition with a similar title has the imprint: "London Printed for and sold by William and Joseph Marshall at the Bible in Newgate Street and at the Bible in Grace-Church Street." This is probably the one announced in the Term Catalogue, Hilary 1696–7, as "sold by W. Marshall at the Bible in Newgate street; and J. Marshall at the Bible in Grace-

Church-street" (*T.C.* III, 9). This edition also contains 14 engraved leaves printed on one side, the right-hand plates being numbered 2, 3, [blank], 5, 6, Finis. Two of the plates used in the first and third editions, beginning "For your ease in writing" and ending "that it may agree with its name", have been re-engraved and the text occupies four pages in this edition. Copies are in B.M.L. (7942.aaa.34); U.L.C. (L.32.51²); R.L.M. (Bailey coll., 514.L.2); C.L.M. (Byrom coll., 3F.1.10); N.L.S. (Warden coll., Wn.1756); P.L.L.; L.N.Y. (Beale coll., *IDS p.v.18, no. 5); U.L.Y. (Z81.15); Boston Public Library, Boston, Mass.; S.L.D.; and W.J.C.

An edition with a similar title has the imprint: "London Printed for and sold by William and Joseph Marshall at the Bible in Newgate Street." A copy is in W.J.C. This is perhaps the edition announced in the Term Catalogue, Hilary 1701, as "Printed for W. Marshall at the Bible in Newgate street" (*T.C.* III, 236), or one of the reprints announced as "Printed for W. and J. Marshall at the Bible in Newgate street" in the Term Catalogues dated Trinity 1703 (*T.C.* III, 362), Michaelmas 1704 (*T.C.* III, 431), Hilary 1705 (*T.C.* III, 446), Trinity 1706 (*T.C.* III, 518) and Trinity 1707 (*T.C.* III, 562).

In the later editions of "Rich Redivivus" the plates are much worn, the shorthand characters in the shilling space at the top of the title-page have become illegible and the date has been partially or wholly obliterated.

Stringer's system purports to be an improvement on that of Rich, but the alphabet is identical and all the defects of the original are retained.

NATHANIEL STRINGER (fl. 1676) appears to have sprung from an old Yorkshire family of that name. According to Alexander Paterson, he was "probably a native of Sharlston, near Wakefield, where numerous branches of the Stringer family long resided, and were of sufficient importance to possess a coat of arms, which the stenographer ostentatiously displays on his title-page" (*Phonetic Journal*, vol. LXV, p. 317, 21 April 1906). The armorial bearings in question appear to be: Arms: three eaglets erminois; Crest: a griffin's head erminois. As Mr A. T. Wright has pointed out, they are an approximation to the arms and crest claimed by George Stringer, or Stringer, merchant, at the Visitation of London, 1633, in respect of his descent from Thomas Stringer of Whiston, Yorkshire (*Jeremiah Rich*, 1911, p. 88*n.*). The statement that Stringer's arms are the same as Jeremiah Rich's (J. Westby Gibson's *Bibliography of Shorthand*, 1887, p. 213) is unsupported by evidence. Nathaniel, son of William and Susan Stringer, was baptised on 17 June 1647 at St Mary Woolchurch Haw, London, and buried there four days later. The stenographer may well have been another son of the same parents, born subsequently, on whom the same Christian name was bestowed.

The engraved portrait by Drapentier prefixed to Stringer's book of 1676 is that of a man of no very mature age. The fact that he describes himself on the title-page of this work as a quondam scholar of Jeremiah Rich (see p. 63) and begins his address to the reader with a reference to Rich as "my quondam Master" suggests that he had received personal tuition from that worthy.

Short Writing, | *Begun by Nature;* | *Compleated by Art* | *Manifesting the Irregu-* | *larity of placeing the Artificial be-* | *fore the Natural or Symbolical* | *Contractions;* | And | *Proposing a Method more suited to* | *Sense, and more fully answering ŷ* | *Requisites of a Compleat Character,* | *in the shortning both of Words and* | *Sentences.* | *Invented, Taught &* *Published* | *with Plaine Directions, Examples* | *and a Specimen of the Writing* | *By* | *Laurence Steel* | *Sold in Bristoll by the* | *Author, &* *also by Charles Allen,* | *Bookseller in Broad-street of the same* | *Citty: And in London by Benja-* | *min Clark Stationer, in* | *George Court* | *Lumbard* | *Street And others.* | *Printed in the Yeare* 1678. | *Joseph: Browne: Sculpsit.*   [860⁸.]

7 × 3⅞ in., 8vo, 20 leaves engraved throughout and printed on one side only. Title within architectural border. No headlines to pages. No signatures. No colophon.

Leaf 1ᵃ Title, 1ᵇ blank, 2ᵃ An Explanation of the Title and Method, 2ᵇ blank, 3ᵃ The Table of Emblems, 3ᵇ blank, 4ᵃ Table (continued), 4ᵇ blank, 5ᵃ Table (contd.), 5ᵇ blank, 6ᵃ Table (contd.), 6ᵇ blank, 7ᵃ Table (contd.), 7ᵇ blank, 8ᵃ Table (contd.), 8ᵇ blank, 9ᵃ Contractions of sentences, terminations, etc., 9ᵇ blank, 10ᵃ Contractions and examples, 10ᵇ blank, 11ᵃ Alphabet, Contractions, etc., 11ᵇ blank, 12ᵃ Double consonants, etc., 12ᵇ blank, 13ᵃ Contractions, 13ᵇ blank, 14ᵃ Contractions, etc., 14ᵇ blank, 15ᵃ Vowels' places and examples of long words, 15^b blank, 16^a Phonetic writing and examples of omissions of vowels, 16^b blank, 17^a Contractions by prefixes, tenses and persons, 17^b blank, 18^a Contractions with negative and interrogative, 18^b blank, 19^a Examples, 19^b blank, 20^a Brief specimen of the writing and exercises for learners, 20^b blank.

This is probably the first edition of Steel's shorthand treatise, although 1672 has been suggested as the date of its publication and Steel is mentioned as a shorthand author in Coles's work of 1674 (see p. 87). It was announced under "Miscellanies" in the Term Catalogue, Hilary 1678/9 (*T.C.* 1, 342). Copies of this edition are in B.M.L. (Fraser coll., 1042.b.62.(1)); B.L.O. (Lewis coll., 302.g.152.(11)); C.L.M. (Harland coll., Mun.D.1.89); R.L.M. (Bailey coll., 514.K.100); and W.J.C. An imperfect copy is in C.L.W. (Walford coll.).

The Bodleian Library contains a copy (50.c.14.(2)) agreeing with the Pepysian copy, but with an additional letterpress title-page prefixed dated 1679 and six pages of letterpress introduction "To the Reader". The letterpress title reads: "A New Method of Short-Writing. Furnished with Variety of Pleasant Helps to the Memory, from Nature, Reason and Art. Whereby Matters may be taken or copied out in the time they are spoken or read over, to the great Ease of Parents and Masters, and the saving about five parts in six of the Labour and Time that is usually required in long-hand. Published for the Advantage of Youth and others, in my Book, entituled, *Short-Writing begun by Nature, compleated by Art*. Engraven in Copper, and sold in Books and Sheets by *Benjamin Clark* Stationer in *George-Yard* in *Lumbard-Street* in *London*. And by *Charles Allen* Bookseller in *Broadstreet* in *Bristol*, and others. To which are now added those Encouragements and Directions which I have usually given in teaching, for the speedy attaining of it without the Help of any other Tutor than the Book. *Performed by* Laurence Steel. Printed in the Year 1679."

An undated edition, with the same title and contents as that of 1678, but with a different imprint, is in L.C.W. (Z56.S814). The imprint reads: "*London Printed, and | Sold by* T. Sowle *in White- | hart Court Gracious Street, | Also Sold at ƴ Bible in George- | yard Lombard Street. | Where may be had Stationary | Wares of all Sorts Wholesale | or Retail at Reasonable Rates*". This apparently unique copy has a MS. note: "The only copy I have met with. W. Blair 1808." and another note referring to the 1678 edition. Tace Sowle, the printer, issued books from White Hart Court between 1694 and 1706. (See W. J. Carlton's *Laurence Steel, an Old-Time Quaker Stenographer*, 1928.)

A reprint was announced in the Term Catalogue, Hilary 1697–8, as "Sold at Bristoll by the Author, and Charles Allen Bookseller there. In London by A. and J. Churchill in Pater-noster-row, and B. Clarke in George-yard" (*T.C.* III, 57). No copy of an edition with this imprint has been located.

In constructing his shorthand alphabet, Steel followed closely the lines laid down by John Willis and Henry Dix, but he rejected the customary method of "teaching to write first by the letters and vowels' places" in favour of "the ready expressing of words by their natural and proper emblems", thus subordinating the alphabet to a more or less arbitrary symbolism. This error of judgment was fatal to the success of his system in point of practical utility. He divided his manual into three parts, the first comprising words and sentences with their "significant emblems", the second words not expressible by emblems, the third teaching "a new invention for the more effectual contracting of sentences like words".

Steel's emblem-writing must have imposed a heavy strain on those who strove to master it, but one or two features of his method entitle it to be ranked above the common level of most contemporary systems. Elisha Coles has pointed out that Steel was the first to restrict the vowels' places to three, and it seems likely that Mason, who adopted this plan in *Arts Advancement* (1682), was indebted for it to Steel. Although the credit of the idea has been assigned to others, Steel also appears to have been the first to attempt to methodise the auxiliary verbs, and he used the circle as an extra-alphabetical character to facilitate the joining of certain consonants. Some of his emblems are exceedingly curious. One expressive symbol by which the Quakers were denoted in shorthand treatises of the time—a *q* with a tremulous appendage—finds no place in Steel's list, but with ready resourcefulness he transferred the quivering tail to *d* and made it do duty for "drunkard"!

LAURENCE STEEL (1644–1684) was born in London about 1644. His parents, who were Independents apparently in easy circumstances, dedicated him to the ministry, and at an early age strong religious convictions caused him acute distress of mind. Dissatisfied with the Presbyterians and Independents (among whom he seems to have preached as a young man), he travelled many miles in search of a body with whom he felt he could unite, and after attending several Quaker meetings joined the Society of Friends in September 1673 (*Journal of George Fox*, ed. N. Penney, 1911, II, 323). Soon after this decisive event in his career he left the Dorsetshire family where he had been engaged as chaplain and tutor to the children. Received by his relatives, he "kept to Friends' meetings, waiting in silence for about twelve months, and then broke forth sometimes in a few words of prayer, and sometimes of exhortation, and so grew and encreased in his gift, till he had an eminent testimony, and well accepted" (J. Whiting's *Persecution Expos'd*, 1715, p. 118).

In the spring of 1674 Steel settled in Bristol and "kept school in the great Meeting House in the Friers", a room being allotted for this purpose over the meeting house. His name recurs frequently in the records of the Bristol Meeting, chiefly in connection with the preparation of papers on questions of "discipline", and he is said to have been "very serviceable in that city and country adjacent". In 1677 appeared "Jacob the Plain Man Wrestling with God", an introspective autobiography in which some of Steel's earlier spiritual experiences are narrated. He was one of half-a-dozen local Friends who put their names to a printed broadside, dated 6 May 1678, containing "Advice to the youth of friends in relation to marriage", which was read by Steel in the public meeting and of which 500 copies were distributed.

The inclusion of Steel's name among "Authors of Short-hand", as well as his alphabet and method of vowel indication, in Coles's book of 1674 (see p. 87), points to his shorthand system having then existed in manuscript, and it may be that he taught it in the meeting-house school, though no evidence of this has been found. The earliest-known edition of "Short Writing", dated 1678, was licensed for publication in February 1678/9. The author, who declared his readiness to give instruction in the art, was to be heard of "at the Widdow Heli's upon the Wair in Bristol".

During the imprisonment of his friend John Whiting in 1679, Steel had many meetings in Whiting's house at Nailsea, and in the following year visited him in prison at Ilchester. About this time a bitter intestine controversy was agitating the West of England Friends, to which Steel contributed a work entitled "Esau Supplanted", apparently unpublished. Writing to George Fox in 1681, he asked for the return of his MS. Complaining of pain and weakness in his head, he added: "Bristol is like to be a place eminent for persecution wch ripens more & more." This prediction was quickly verified, and although Steel had been deputed to keep watch over the door of the meeting house, it was raided on 14 December by the mob, headed by the town clerk, three militia officers and a number of constables. A distress of £5 was demanded of Laurence Steel, "who dwelt in a Tenement over ye Meeting Room", and as he did not immediately comply the place was rifled, windows smashed, seats and forms seized, and galleries torn down. This exploit was renewed later, a bed and other household goods being thrown down into the meeting room from the tenement, as well as the school benches, forms, chairs and a table.

From this time forward the Bristol Quakers were the victims of continual persecution, their meetings being brutally disturbed, their property damaged and heavy fines imposed. They were crowded into the prisons until there was no more room for them, and at length, remonstrances proving of no avail, Laurence Steel and Charles Jones, jun., travelled to London to lay their grievances before the king. In London they were joined by George Whitehead, who secured their admittance to the royal presence and has left an account of the episode (*Christian Progress*, 1725, pp. 504–13). On 17 February 1681/2 the three indomitable Friends pleaded before the king and council for three-quarters of an hour with their hats on their heads, their scruples in this regard being respected. Whitehead was the chief spokesman, but Steel gave his testimony as an eyewitness of the insults offered to and the cruel wrongs inflicted upon himself and his comrades, and he laid a detailed statement of their case on the council table. The result was an order directing the Bristol magistrates to enquire into and redress the "Streightness and Noysomness of the Prison of Newgate", but the meetings of all the dissenters in the city continued to be violently disturbed, and the Quakers, forcibly kept out of their meeting house, assembled in the adjoining court. Steel was singled out for special molestation as one who had taken an active part in seeking redress at the hands of the king, and on 18 September 1682 was himself imprisoned in Newgate gaol, Bristol "for meeting". In a list drawn up in the following November his name occur as a prisoner in the "Chapell Chamber", with twelve other Friends, one of them a boy of 15 (J. Besse's *Collection of the Sufferings of the People called Quakers*, 1753, 1, 66, 67). Towards the end of 1683 he was again imprisoned for six months under the Conventicle Act, and subjected to the most barbarous treatment by the gaoler, Isaac Dennis. Five of his fellow-prisoners succumbed for want of air and room.

When released from his confinement, it was with a constitution, which had never been strong, greatly impaired. He was no longer able to attend the meetings of Friends but grew gradually weaker and died, a martyr for his faith, at the age of 40. John Whiting has left on record, in "Persecution Expos'd", some personal details of the Quaker stenographer. "About this time [1684] our dear Friend Lawrence Steel, of Bristol, died, though not in Prison; yet not long after he was released. In a Sence of the Loss of whom (being one I dearly loved, and was well acquainted with) I write a few Lines as a Testimony concerning him.... He was a comely Person, but pale Complexioned, being inclined to a Dropsie, and infirm as to his Health, which no doubt was heightned, and his Health impaired by his close Confinement in Newgate; and did not live long after his Releasement (at the end of six Months) but died of a Diabetis, about the tenth (being buried the 12th) of the eighth Month [i.e. October] 1684, laying down his Head in Peace with the Lord. He was a Man of grave solid serious Deportment; of a sweet even Temper and Disposition; of a sedate retired Life; and very Exemplary in his Conversation, in which he walked as a Stranger and Pilgrim on Earth, but hath finished his Course, and kept the Faith, and receiv'd the Crown of Life; and hath left a good Savour behind him; of whose Sincerity and Integrity to God and his Truth, I could write much, but his innocent Life and Testimony is the best Memorial of him, and his Memory is blessed."

By his will, which he is said to have made in prison, Steel left £120 to be disbursed among the Quaker poor and Quaker prisoners of Bristol. The money was first lent out at interest, and afterwards invested in the building of the Friends' workhouse, erected in 1698, on which it was secured by way of mortgage with other legacies by deed poll dated 25 September 1701.

(W. J. Carlton's *Laurence Steel, an Old-time Quaker Stenographer*, reprinted from *The Journal of the Friends' Historical Society*, 1928.)

Stenographia | *or* | *The Art of* Short-writing *compleated* | *in a far more Compendious method* | *than any yet extant* | *By W*ᵐ *Addy* | *Writing M*ʳ | London *Printed for ẙ Author* | *Sold by Dorman Newman at the Kings Armes in the Poultry and* | *Samuel Crouch at the Flower de luce in Cornhill* | *William Marshall at the Bible in Newgate street* | *Tho: Cockerill at ẙ* 3 *Leggs over against the Stocks Market and* | *I. Lawrence at ẙ Angel in the Poultry.* [860³.]

6⅞ × 4¼ in., 8vo, 9 double-page engraved plates (numbered 1 to 9), consisting of frontispiece portrait of Addy by J. Sturt after S. Barker and pictorial title-page (1 plate), verses to the author signed N. H. and C. N., and Addy's address "To the candid and ingenious reader" (1 plate); text (7 plates): total, 18 leaves, printed on one side. N.D. (1693?).

This is probably the edition of Addy's "Stenographia" announced in the Term Catalogue, Hilary 1692/3, as "now reprinted; and sold by J. Lawrence at the Angel in the Poultrey" (*T.C.* II, 445).

The original marbled wrappers are preserved in the Pepysian copy, which has, however, been cut down by the binder to 6½ × 3¾ in., taking away the numbers on the plates. In some copies the space in the lower right-hand corner of plate 5 contains instructions for indicating the three persons; in the Pepysian copy this space is blank.

Other copies are in B.M.L. (1042.b.80, with autograph of James Campbell, 1692); U.L.C. (Hh.14.30); G.L.L. (C.8.4); C.L.W.; L.N.Y. (Beale coll., *IDS p.v.65, no. 10); U.L.Y.; and W.J.C.

The first edition of "Stenographia" appears to have been published in 1684, and was announced in the Term Catalogue, Trinity 1684, as "Sold by D. Newman at the King's Arms in the Poultrey, and S. Crouch at the Flower de luce in Cornhill, and W. Marshall at the Bible in Newgate street" (*T.C.* II, 87). The Carlton collection includes a copy of Sturt's engraved title-page (Johnson, No. 2), with the above imprint, followed by: "Who please for their greater expedition may be taught by the Author who is to be spoken with at Mʳ Newman's, at ẙ Place above mentioned."

Another edition has the imprint: "Printed for ẙ Author. Sold by Wᵐ Marshall at ẙ Bible in Newgate street. Who please for their greater expedition may be taught by the Author who is to be spoken with at Mʳ Marshall's, at ẙ Place above mentioned." Copies are in L.C.W. (Z56.A23) and S.L.D. (C.a.11).

Another edition has the imprint: "Printed for Iohn Lawrence at the Angel in the Poultry over against the Counter where are sold the Short-hand Bibles. 1695." This edition is announced in the Term Catalogue, Trinity 1695 (*T.C.* II, 560). Copies are in B.M.L. (7942.aaa.41); B.L.O. (8° D.112Art); C.L.M. (Harland coll., Mun.D1.86); N.L.S. (Warden coll., Wn.824); I.P.L. (Taylor coll.); B.N.P. (Rés.V.2456); S.L.D. (C.a.11); L.N.Y. (*IDS p.v.19, no. 2, and Heffley coll., *IDS p.v.230, no. 7); C.E.B. (Havette coll.); and W.J.C.

A reprint was announced in the Term Catalogue, Michaelmas 1696 (*T.C.* II, 606).

An edition without date bears the imprint: "Printed for Aaron Ward, at the Kings Arms in Little Britain, where may be had a great Variety of other Short Hand Books." The only copy known is in P.L.L. (O'Donnell coll.). Aaron Ward published books from this address between 1724 and 1747.

The system of shorthand expounded in Addy's "Stenographia" is that of Jeremiah Rich (see p. 62), whose alphabet he adopted and to whom he acknowledged his indebtedness in these terms: "The Embrio...I ow the Ingenious Mʳ Rich, whose principles I coveted rather an improvement of, then to raise a fabrick *de Novo.*"

In his address to the reader Addy wrote: "If ŵ I entertaine the with here, find a friendly welcome, thou mayest expect (as soon as ẙ undertaking can be finished) to see the Holy Bible containing the Old & New Testament Printed in the same Character." The promised work duly appeared in 1687—see next entry.

[The] Holy Bible containing | [the] Old and New Testament with [the] Singing Psalms | in short hand written by William Addy | [Ornament] | Colossians 3. 16. Let the word of Christ dwell in you richly in all wisdom | [Six more lines of shorthand] | 1687. [**10.**]

The above is in shorthand characters at the top of a pictorial title-page of architectural design representing Moses and Aaron with two tablets between them on which are the Ten Commandments in shorthand. At the foot of this page is: "The Bible engraven by John Sturt", also in shorthand. The imprint at the foot of leaf 5ᵇ reads:

London *Printed for the Author,* | *and Peter Story. and sold by,* | *Tho: Fabian at the Bible in Pauls Church* | *yard. Dorman Newman at ỹ. King's Armes* | *in the Poultry. Sam: Crouch at ỹ. Flower* | *de-luce in Cornhill. Wᵐ Marshall at the* | *Bible in Newgate street. Thomas Cockerill* | *at ỹ. 3 Leggs over against ỹ Stocks Market* | *I. Lawrence at ỹ. Angel in ỹ. Poultry.*

4½ × 3 in., 12mo, pp. (10) + 278 + (6) + 80 (numbered 279–358) + (2) + 38 (numbered 359–396) + (4), engraved throughout in shorthand, save the imprint which is in longhand; borders and columns rubricated by hand. The Bible is printed in two columns, the metrical Psalms in three.

Leaves 1ᵃ–2ᵃ blank, 2ᵇ Portrait of Addy by J. Sturt with name "Gulielmus Addy" and four lines of shorthand below signed "S. P.", 3ᵃ Title, 3ᵇ blank, 4ᵃ Preface, 4ᵇ–5ᵃ blank, 5ᵇ List of abbreviations and imprint, 6ᵃ–144ᵇ Old Testament, 145ᵃ–146ᵇ blank, 147ᵃ Engraving of the four Evangelists seated at a table with tablets and pens: in shorthand "The New Testament of our Lord and Saviour Jesus Christ", 147ᵇ blank, 148ᵃ–187ᵇ New Testament, 188ᵃ Engraving of King David playing a harp: in shorthand "Psalms of David in metre", 188ᵇ blank, 189ᵃ–207ᵇ Psalms, 208ᵃ–208ᵇ blank save for rubrication, 209ᵃ–209ᵇ blank.

This is the first edition of Addy's, the earliest complete Bible printed in shorthand, with Sternhold and Hopkins' metrical version of the Psalms. The system employed is that of Jeremiah Rich as expounded in Addy's "Stenographia" (see p. 104). This edition was announced in the Term Catalogue, Trinity 1687, as follows: "The Holy Bible, containing the Old and New Testament, together with the Singing Psalms; all done upon Copper-plates, and in Short-hand, by William Addy. Twelves. Sold by T. Fabian at the Bible in St. Paul's Churchyard" (*T.C.* II, 198).

The Pepysian copy is in the original red morocco binding, with gilt tooling on back and sides. Pepys's portrait bookplate is pasted on leaf 3^b and his "anchor" bookplate on leaf 208^a. Some copies exhibit slight variations in the arrangement of the preliminary leaves. One of two copies in B.M.L. (C.65.h.7) has the following MS. note on a vellum sheet pasted in at the end: "This Bible in Stenography my Brethren at sight, and all others Skill'd in ỹ Art of Sculpture know it's Engraven; but in a Peculiar Manner. It was written by Mr Addy in ungum'd Ink burnished on the wax and then run thrô with the Engraver by John Sturt." The copy in U.L.C. (LE.22.1) is bound in dark green morocco, elaborately tooled, and bears the inscription "Bibliothecae Acad: Cantab: Authoris donum. 1687". The copy in B.L.O. (8° G.279.Th.) has the inscription "Given by Mr. John Sturt, the Graver. June 18, 1698". Other copies are in the Library of the British and Foreign Bible Society, London (H.C.638.(3)); R.L.M. (514.E.10 and 12); C.L.M. (Mun.D.1.56); N.L.S. (Warden coll., Wn.878); L.N.Y. (Beale coll., *KC); U.L.Y. (Healey coll., F25.366); and W.J.C.

The second edition of Addy's Bible is similar to the first in every respect, except that leaf 4^b contains Addy's dedication in shorthand to William III (who landed at Torbay 5 Nov. 1688 and was proclaimed king 13 Feb. 1688–9) in place of the list of abbreviations, while the imprint at the foot of leaves 4^b and 5^a reads: "*London Printed for the Author, and sold by Dorman | Newman at the Kings Armes in ỹ Poultry Tho Fabian | in Pauls Church yard Sam: Crouch at ỹ Flower | de luce in Cornhill Wm Marshall at ỹ Bible in | Newgate street Tho: Cockerill at ỹ 3 Leggs over against ỹ | Stocks market I. Lawrence at ỹ Angel in ỹ Poultry &^ct*". Copies are in B.M.L. (1159.b.22); R.L.M. (514.E.11); L.N.Y. (Beale coll., Reserve); and W.J.C.

The third edition is similar to the second, but the dedication and preface have been re-engraved and exhibit slight variations, while the imprint at the foot of leaf 5^a reads: "*Sold by* I. Lawrence *at ỹ* Angel | *in the* Poultry." This edition was probably issued about 1696, as the Term Catalogue for Michaelmas of that year refers to "the Shorthand Bibles, likewise newly reprinted" (*T.C.* II, 606). Copies are in R.L.M. (514.E.9); N.L.S. (Warden coll., Wn.880, portrait and title-page in facsimile); and W.J.C.

WILLIAM ADDY is the subject of a short article in the *D.N.B.* by Mr Thompson Cooper, F.S.A. No biographical information concerning him is given there, however. In "The Addy Family of Darton and Elsewhere in the West Riding" (*Yorkshire Archaeological Journal*, vol. XXVII), Mr S. O. Addy, M.A., suggests a possible identification of the London writing master with William Addy, baptised at Wath-upon-Dearne in 1618, third son of John Addy, then clerk of that parish. If so, he would have been sixty-six when his "Stenographia" was first published and sixty-nine when his shorthand Bible appeared.

The Pepysian Library contains an "Alphabetical List of the surviving Maister-Pen-Men of England, and more particularly in and about the Citys of London and Westminster, in the year 1699", in Pepys's hand. The first name in the list is "Addy, Talbot-Court in Fenchurch-Street, Disciple of Mr. Story". "Mr. Story" is doubtless the Peter Story whose name appears on the title-page of the first edition of Addy's Bible and whose abode is given in Pepys's list as St Lawrence Poultney Hill. William Massey says that Story "was reckoned a fine penman in his time" (*The Origin and Progress of Letters*, 1763, p. 147). The "Calligraphicall Collection" in the Pepysian Library (vol. II, p. 260) contains a specimen of his art inscribed "To the worthily honored and most ingenious Conserver of Art and Science Samuell Pepys Esqr this specimen of ẙ art of writing is presented by his Servt Pr Story".

Mr S. O. Addy writes (*op. cit.*, p. 174): "It is tempting to suggest that the letters S. P. under the verses on Addy's two portraits are the initials of Samuel Pepys. But I dare not do that, even though in his Diary on the 25th of March, 1666, he tells us that he wrote Latin verse at school. He was certainly capable of doing so, and the writing of such verse is an art which, once acquired, is never forgotten....On 9 Nov. 1660, Pepys, who was then living in Seething Lane, writes that he dined 'with Mr. Wivell at the Hoop Tavern, where we had Mr. Shepley, Talbot, Adams, Mr. Chaplin and Osborne, and our dinner given to us by Mr. Ady and another, Mr. Wine, the King's fishmonger'.... It is possible that this "Mr. Ady" was William Addy, the stenographer, written in southern spelling." Mr F. McD. C. Turner has pointed out, however, that "Mr. Ady" in Wheatley's edition of the *Diary* is an error for Mr Adis (*The Times*, 23 Feb. 1933).

In dedicating his shorthand Bible to William III, Addy described himself as "a sharer in the deliverance whereof your Majesty was the glorious instrument" and stated that the work was the product of "some years' elaborate study and pains". The preface "to the pious and ingenious reader" concludes: "I shall not need here to demonstrate the comprehensive utility, as well as the rarity (the like having never been done before) of what I have offered to thine acceptation (viz.) the Holy Bible in stenography; how grateful it will be to some (especially those more refined spirits and pious inclinations who do not only give every worthy undertaking verbal compliment, but have put to their hands in promoting this work by subscription), to whom, if I were not confined by some who desire not publication of their own praise, I would otherwise have showed my respect....For the censures of some I believe I shall not want, but the pleasure I take in serving upon the public and finding a free and fair reception amongst the more judicious and wiser sort of mankind, will countervail over all the impertinent cavils of the ignorant, and likewise the unwearied pains of him who looks upon it as the greatest privilege to lay out his talent for God, and his country's service—William Addy." The dedication and preface were reprinted in full in *The Willis-Byrom Club Bulletin*, ii, 27–8, 35–6, 1916.

(*D.N.B.*; Sir Ambrose Heal's *The English Writing-Masters and their Copy-Books*, 1931, p. 3; S. O. Addy's *The Addy Family of Darton and Elsewhere in the West Riding*, 1923.)

Short =hand yet shorter: | or, | The Art of Short-Writing | advanced in a more swift, easie, | regular, and natural Method than | hitherto. | Whereby | The former Difficulties in placing the | Vowels are removed; they, the Dip- | thongs and Consonants, further con- | tracted; the Particles, Pronouns, De- | grees of Comparison, Persons, Moods, | Tenses, Contrarieties, Repetitions, Sen- | tences Negative and Interrogatory are | shortned. | The Rules are plain, easie to be remembred and | applied to any other *Short-hand*, that such as | have learned other Authors may have hence | a very considerable help to write more swiftly | without altering their Foundation. | By George Ridpath. | *If any desire to be expeditiously taught, the Author* | *may be heard of in* Eagle and Child Court *in* | St. Giles *in the Fields*, *near the Church, or upon the* | *Scots Walk at Exchange-time most Saturdays.* | *London*, Printed by *J. D.* for the Author, 1687.   [860⁷.]

6¾×4 in., pp. (4)+43 letterpress, with 2 folding engraved plates. In the right-hand lower corner of plate 2 is "R Simson sculp:". No headlines to pages. Sign. A–C8 in eights.

Leaf 1ᵃ Title, 1ᵇ blank, 2ᵃ–2ᵇ Dedication "To the Right Honourable Philip Lord Wharton, Baron of Wharton", 3ᵃ–6ᵃ Address to the Courteous Reader, 6ᵃ–24ᵃ Text, 24ᵇ blank.

This is the first edition of Ridpath's shorthand manual. It was announced in *The London Gazette*, No. 2329, 12–15 March 1687–8, as follows: "☞ Short-hand yet Shorter. By George Ridpath. Being the best Method for teaching the said Art yet Extant; with Rules for the help of such as have learned other Authors, and desire to write more swiftly. Price 1s. Sold by Mr. Crouch in Popes-Head-Alley, Mr. Taylor at the Ship in St. Paul's Churchyard, Mr. Harrison at Lincolns-Inn Gate, Mr. Fox at the Angel in Westminster-hall, and the Author in Eagle and Child Court, St. Giles's in the Fields, who also teaches the Latin Tongue much sooner than ordinary." Other copies are in B.M.L. (51.b.15); C.L.M. (Byrom coll., 2.I.3.25); R.L.M. (Bailey coll., 514.K.54); N.L.S. (Warden coll., Wn.863); L.C.W. (Z56.R547 Office); L.N.Y. (Beale coll., IDS p.v.65, no. 5); U.L.Y. (Healey coll., F25.356); and W.J.C.

An edition was published in 1696 with the imprint: "*London*, Printed for *Andrew Bell*, at the Cross-Keys in the *Poultrey* near Stocks-Market, 1696." Copies are in B.M.L. (Blair coll., 7942.b.26) and W.J.C. (wanting leaf A2).

Ridpath claimed to have paid special attention to distinctness and facility of joining in composing his alphabet, but it included several of the compound characters of his predecessors. He provided alternative signs for *s*. Initial and final vowels were indicated by a dot in the vowel's place, medial vowels by the "mode". The omission of certain prepositions and auxiliary verbs could be implied by the relative positions of the preceding and following words, and a similar device was employed to indicate the moods and tenses. An original feature of the system is the intersection of two consonants to indicate *ar, er, ir, or, ur*. The work concludes with a long list of "analogical marks" or symbolical characters for words and phrases.

GEORGE RIDPATH (166–?–1726), Scottish nationalist and journalist, whose biography occupies five columns in the *D.N.B.*, claimed descent from the Gordons. He was probably a native of Berwickshire and may have been a son of George Readpath, who inherited land from his father Thomas in 1654. He spent his youth with his mother at Colbrandspath, where he appears to have been educated before going to Edinburgh University. In 1681 he was tutor (or, according to his enemies, servant) to the sons of a Mr Gray at Edinburgh. The burning in effigy of the Pope by the students at Christmas led to his arrest as one of the ringleaders. The Clerk to the Council described him as being "not then a boy, but a fellow come to years". He was kept in irons for some days and proclaimed that he was suffering for the Protestant religion. Charged with threatening to burn the Provost's house, he was banished the country after five weeks' imprisonment (*The Scots Episcopal Innocence*, 1694, pp. 52–6). Abandoning an intention to enter the Scottish ministry, he went to London to seek a livelihood by his pen.

In 1687 Ridpath published his "Shorthand yet Shorter" with a dedication to Philip, Lord Wharton, "because it had its birth under your Lordship's roof, while I had the honour to be one of your Lordship's domesticks". The author offered to give lessons in the art and was to be heard of in Eagle and Child Court, St Giles-in-the-Fields, near the Church, or upon the Scots Walk at Exchange-time most Saturdays. In March 1688 he advertised in *The London Gazette* as a teacher of Latin and shorthand in Eagle and Child Court.

Little is known of his activities during the next few years, but soon after the Revolution he was an active London journalist (Carstares's *State Papers*, p. 364). In 1693, under the *nom de plume* Will Laick, he violently attacked the Scottish bishops in "An Answer to the Scotch Presbyterian Eloquence" and "A Continuation of the Answer". An equally virulent retort was made by Dr Alexander Munro in "An Apology for the Clergy of Scotland" and "The Spirit of Calumny and Slander examined, chastised, and exposed, in a Letter to a Malicious Libeller, More particularly addressed to Mr. George Ridpath, newsmonger, near St. Martins-in-the-Fields". Ridpath is called "the head of the Presbyterian Party in Scotland". He replied in "The Scots Episcopal Innocence", 1694, which is chiefly valuable for the autobiographical information it contains, and "The Queries and Protestation of the Scots Episcopal Clergy against the Authority of the Presbyterian General Assemblies", 1694. When the second edition of his shorthand manual was published in 1696, he was acting as a sort of spy on the Bishop of Glasgow and on Dr Munro (*Hist. MSS. Comm.*, 12th Report, VIII, 50).

Ridpath was the inventor of a forerunner of the modern duplicating machine called "polygraphy". It was described as "a writing engine, that one man may with great facility write two, four, six or more copies of any one thing upon so many different sheets of paper at once, of extraordinary use for expediting business, whereof many copies are required". Among the advantages claimed for this machine was that, "being moved by the foot while the hand guides the pens, it keeps the whole body in warmth and exercise, which prevents many of the usual inconveniences of a sedentary life, besides the time which the engine saves in despatch" (Wm. Turner's *Compleat History of the most Remarkable Providences*, 1697, III, 26; John Dunton's *Life and Errors*, 1818, pp. 179, 180).

In 1695 Ridpath published, with a dedication to Secretary Johnston, a translation of Sir Thomas Craig's "Scotland's Sovereignty asserted; being a Dispute concerning Homage", and in 1698 he translated De Souligné's "Political Mischiefs of Popery". In "A Dialogue between Jack and Will, concerning the Lord Mayor's going to Meeting-Houses with the Sword carried before him", 1697, he defended Sir Humphry Edwin, a Presbyterian Lord Mayor; and this was followed in 1699 by "A Roland for an Oliver, or a Sharp Rebuke to a Saucy Levite. In answer to a Sermon preached by Edward Oliver, M.A., before Sir Humphry Edwin. By a Lover of Unity." A book called "The Stage Condemned", in support of Jeremy Collier's "Short View of the Immorality and Profaneness of the English Stage", appeared in 1698, and the author of a reply, "The Stage Acquitted", says it was by "Mr. R[idpa]th, the formidable author of a scandalous newspaper and the wretched retailer of mad Prynne's enthusiastic cant". The name of George Ridpath is found among those who graduated at Edinburgh in 1699 (*Catalogue of Edinburgh Graduates*, 1858, p. 163).

Ridpath's "Scotland's Grievances relating to Darien, humbly offered to the Consideration of Parliament", 1700, contains many strong remarks about a foreign yoke. Next year was published "The Great Reasons and Interests considered anent the Spanish Monarchy", and in 1702 "A Discourse upon the Union of England and Scotland. By a Lover of his Country." In this last work Ridpath opposed the union. In 1703 he published "The Case of Scotsmen residing in England and in the English Plantations" and "A Historical Account of the Ancient Rights and Power of the Parliament of Scotland". These were followed by "An Account of the Proceedings of the Parliament of Scotland", 1703, and "The Reducing of Scotland by Arms...considered", 1705. In a reply to this last pamphlet entitled "Remarks upon a late Dangerous Pamphlet", etc., 1705, the author and publisher are said to have been bound over to appear at the Queen's Bench Bar. In 1706 Ridpath wrote "Considerations upon the Union of the two Kingdoms", which was answered by Sir John Clerk in "A Letter to a Friend, giving an Account how the Treaty of Union has been received here. With Remarks upon what has been written by Mr. H[odges] and Mr. R[idpath]", a piece which has been erroneously attributed to Defoe (*Memoirs of Sir John Clerk*, 1892, p. 244; Lee's *Life of Defoe*, 1867, p. 133).

In 1705 Ridpath assisted James Anderson in the preparation of his "Historical Essay showing that the Crown and Kingdom of Scotland is Imperial and Independent", and in that year he began a correspondence with the Rev. Robert Wodrow, chiefly on the subject of the union and the dreaded episcopal church in Scotland. "The Scots' Representations to Her Majesty, against setting up the Common Prayer-Book in Scotland", 1711, was written, according to a note in the copy in the Scottish National Library, by Ridpath, William Carstares and Defoe. Another piece attributed to Ridpath is "The Oath of Abjuration considered", Edinburgh, 1712. He was employed in correcting Captain Woodes Rogers's "Voyage" (Nichols's *Lit. Anecd.* VIII, 301) and assisted in writing the periodical "History of the Works of the Learned". He contributed to the *Medley* in 1712 (Wilson's *Life of Defoe*, III, 253, 283), and was in constant warfare with the Tory *Post Boy*, published by Abel Roper (Ashton's *Social Life in the Reign of Queen Anne*, II, 72–4). Dunton, a warm admirer, described his style as excellent. "His humility and his honesty have established his reputation. He scorns to receive a farthing of copy-money till he knows what numbers are sold off." For some years he had conducted the Whig journal *The Flying Post or Post-Man*, which according to Dunton was highly valued and sold well, and was described by John Tutchin as "the honestest of all newspapers".

On 8 September 1712 Ridpath was committed to Newgate as the author of three libels in the *Observator*, to which he became a contributor in succession to Tutchin, and in *The Flying Post*, but was released on bail. On 23 October Ridpath and Hunt appeared in the Court of Queen's Bench and were continued on their recognizances. Swift objected to bail being allowed for "the Scotch rogue", who continued to write when at liberty (*Journal to Stella*, 28 Oct. 1712). On 19 February 1713 Ridpath was tried at the Guildhall, the Attorney General declaring that he "had for some years past outwent all his predecessors in scandal". That the trial was largely a party matter is shown by the list of Ridpath's counsel. A collection was made on his behalf, and the Whigs were told that unless they subscribed two guineas they would not be admitted to be members of the party (*Wentworth Papers*, p. 310). The jury found Ridpath guilty of two of the libels, sentence was postponed, and on 1 May his recognizances were estreated because he failed to appear. On 25 May a reward of £100 was offered for his discovery without result, Ridpath having fled to Scotland, and thence to Holland. He now lived at Rotterdam and was referred to in the *Dutch Gazeteer* as one of the best pens in England (Swift's *Works*, 1824, IV, 297). In 1713 he wrote "Some Thoughts concerning the Peace", and in 1714 published a book called "Parliamentary Right Maintained, or the Hanoverian Succession Justified". Copies were sent by different ships to various ports in England, but many were lost or thrown overboard by the captains, who dared not land them, or were returned because no one dared to receive them.

After the accession of George I, Ridpath returned to England and was made one of the patentees for serving the commissioners of the customs in Scotland with stationery wares (*Read's Weekly Journal*, 12 Feb. 1726). In 1717 he was giving Wodrow advice in the preparation of the "History of the Sufferings of the Church of Scotland", and was himself proposing to write a continuation of Buchanan's "Scotch History". *The Flying Post* still waged war with the Tories, and Ridpath made slanderous charges against Nathaniel Mist and others; but in 1719, when he was living in Greville Street, Holborn, he published "An Appeal to the Word of God for the Trinity in Unity". Pope wrote (*Dunciad*, I, 208):

"To Dulness Ridpath is as dear as Mist."

In 1722 he was secretary to a lottery at Harburg, Hanover, in connection with a company formed to maintain trade with that country. The king denied having sanctioned the lottery and a committee of the House of Commons examined

Ridpath in December and January 1723. Most of the company's money had been lost in the South Sea Company and a bill was introduced to suppress the lottery. In February the trustees announced, through Ridpath, that they would return all tickets on application. After this Ridpath avoided old friends, being "under some scandal", and it was alleged that he had been guilty of bigamy. He died on 5 February 1726. By his will of 29 January he left all his estate to his wife Esther, daughter of George Markland, and appointed her sole executrix (P.C.C. 31 Plymouth). His only son, a great help to him in business, died in 1706. Ridpath's papers passed into the hands of Dr James Fraser, one of Wodrow's correspondents. In the memoir of the author prefixed to Wodrow's "History of the Sufferings of the Church of Scotland", Ridpath is said to have been an indefatigable collector of old records and to have possessed one of the largest collections of the kind of any private individual in Great Britain.

Nouvelle | Methode | *ov* | l'Art d'Ecrire | *Aussi vîte qu'on Parle.* | [Woodcut of a globe] | A Paris, | Chez Louys Pralard. | M.DC.XC. [401.]

$5\frac{7}{8} \times 3$ in., pp. 65 + 1 + 82 letterpress, with engraved folding table in six compartments. The running title is "Tacheographie" ("Tacheographia"). Sign. A–A12, ĕ–ĕ 12, ĭ–ĭ 9, A–A3, B–B12, C–C12, D–D12, E–E2.

Leaf 1ᵃ Title in French, 1ᵇ blank, 2ᵃ Title in Latin, 2ᵇ Dedication "Av Roy", 3ᵃ "Lvdovico XIV. Gallorvm & Navarræorum Regi. Pio, Felici, Christianissimo Carolus Aloisius Ramsay N.S.", 3ᵇ–27ᵃ Dedication continued (French and Latin on alternate pages), 27ᵇ Avis au lecteur [Here is the folding table], 28ᵃ Avthor lectori, 28ᵇ–33ᵃ Address to the reader continued (French and Latin on opposite pages), "Dabam Parisiis 9. Decembris anno 1680", 33ᵇ–74ᵇ Text (French and Latin on opposite pages).

The Latin title reads as follows:

Nova | Methodvs | *sive* | ars celeriter. | Et | *compendiose quælibet* | *inter perorandum verba, vt ne vnum* | *quidem excidat describendi.* | [Woodcut of a globe] | Parisiis, | Apud Ludovicum Pralard. | M.DC.XC.

This is one of the later editions of a treatise which, though the author bears a Scottish name, does not seem to have been published in English. It forms the second volume of the Pepysian collection of shorthand books. Other copies are in the Universitäts-Bibliothek, Breslau; Stadtbibliothek, Hamburg; Universitäts-Bibliothek, Munich; Herzogliche Bibliothek, Wolfenbüttel; C.E.B. (Havette coll.); and W.J.C.

Ramsay's shorthand manual was, according to his own statement, "zum ersten mahl in den wöchentlichen Zeitungen einsetzen und publiciren lassen" in August or September 1678 at Frankfurt-am-Main; but this may only mean that its publication was announced in the newspapers. In 1678 it was printed in German and Latin in two small volumes of 30 pages and 1 plate. The German title reads: "Tacheographia. Oder Geschwinde Schreibe-Kunst vermittelst welcher Ein jedweder die Teutsche Spraache so geschwinde schreiben kan als selbe mag geredet werden. Allen Kunstbegierigen zu liebe aufs Kürtzeste verfasset und an den Tag gegeben. Gedruckt im Jahr 1679." The only clue to the author is found in the lower right-hand corner of the engraved plate at the end of the book: "Authore C. A. R. Sumptibus Johannis Georgij Cheeus. Anno. 1678, Frankofurti ad Mœnum." This was the first independent manual of stenography printed in the German language. A copy of the original German edition is in the University Library, Breslau, and a copy of the original Latin edition in the Library of the Stenographischer Gymnasiasterverein nach Stolze, Zeitz. Facsimile reproductions of both were issued in 1904 by the Akademischer Stenographenverein nach Stolze-Schrey, Berlin.

An unauthorised edition, of which no copy is known to be extant, appears to have been issued at Dresden in 1678 by Daniel Hartnach. It is referred to by Ramsay in the preface to his next publication, issued early in 1679 with the following title: "Caroli Aloisii Ramsay New vermehrte Tacheographia. Oder Beschwinde [sic] Schreib-Kunst vermittelst welcher Ein jedweder die Teutsche Sprache so geschwinde schreiben kan als selbe mag geredet werden. Von dem Authore selbsten auffs neuwe durchsehen, verbessert, von allen Fehleren gereiniget und in wenig Regulen verfasset. Benebenst einem angehenckten Unterricht. Wie man durch eine kleine Ubung gantz geschwinde zu dieser Kunst gelangen mag. Leipzig, bey

Johann Fritzschen, 1679." Copies of this 1679 edition are in B.M.L. (1043.b.75) and the Stadtbibliothek, Hamburg.

Another unauthorised German edition, without any author's or printer's name on the title-page, and reproducing the text of the original of 1678, is dated 1679. Copies are in S.L.D.; W.J.C.; Stadtbibliothek, Hamburg; Universitäts-Bibliothek, Breslau; Universitäts-Bibliothek, Erlangen; Hof- und Staatsbibliothek, Munich; Öffentliche Bibliothek, Stuttgart; Kgl. Niederländische Bibliothek, Leyden; Library of the Gabelsberger Stenographenverein, Prague.

Another Latin edition, with the author's name on the title-page, bears the imprint: "*Francof. et Lipsiæ. Apud Johannem Bielckium Bibl. Jenensis. Aº 1681.*" Copies are in S.L.D.; W.J.C.; Königliche Öffentliche Bibliothek, Dresden; Herzogliche Bibliothek, Gotha; Stadtbibliothek, Hamburg; Stadtbibliothek, Cologne; Hof- und Staatsbibliothek, Munich; Stadtbibliothek, Stralsund; Grossherzogliche Bibliothek, Weimar; Herzogliche Bibliothek, Wolfenbüttel; Royal Library, Leyden; Library of the Dutch Literary Society, Leyden.

The earliest edition in French and Latin is dated 1681. The first title reads: "Tacheographie ou l'Art d'Escrire aussi viste qu'on parle. *Renfermé sous trés-peu de preceptes; Le tout enseigné par une methode briefve & fort intelligible, expliquée par plusieurs exemples.* Par le Sieur Charles Al. Ramsay, Gentil-homme Escossois. *Mis en lumiere pour l'usage des Theologiens, Iurisconsultes, Gens qui font profession des Lettres, Medecins, Estudians, & de tous ceux qui font des Recueils de Sermons, & autres pieces d'eloquence.* Traduit depuis peu de Latin en François par le sieur A. D. G. A̾ Paris, Se vend chez l'Autheur, ruë Dauphine, au bout du Pont-neuf, à l'Image S. Pierre, chez un Bourelier. M.DC.LXXXI. *Avec Privilege du Roy.*" On the verso is the Latin title: "Tacheographia seu Ars Celeriter et *compendiosè quælibet inter perorandum verba, ut ne unum quidem excidat, describendi.* Præceptis paucis comprehensa, idque methodo brevi ac perspiscua tradita, plurimisque exemplis illustrata. *Opera Caroli Alois Ramsay Nobilis Scoti.* In bonum usum Theologorum, ICtorum, Scribarum, Medicorum, omniumque studiosorum, necnon concionum auditorum singularem gratiam, in lucem edita. *Parisiis excvdebat. Cvm Privilegio.*"

Copies are in B.M.L. (1043.b.76); B.N.P.; P.L.L. (O'Donnell coll.); S.L.D.; Universitäts-Bibliothek, Jena; Town Library, Lyons; Hof- und Staatsbibliothek, Munich; L.C.W.; L.N.Y. (Beale coll.); C.L.M.; N.L.S. (Warden coll., Wn.3786); C.E.B. (Havette coll.); and W.J.C. The dedication copy to Louis XIV, with the royal arms of France on the sides, was sold at Sotheby's auction rooms on 11 June 1902.

Another edition in French and Latin, with similar titles, is dated 1683. Copies are in B.M.L. (1043.a.46); B.L.O. (302.g.152.(3)); R.L.M. (Bailey coll., 514.K.62); Universitäts-Bibliothek, Breslau; Königliche Öffentliche Bibliothek, Dresden; Universitäts-Bibliothek, Göttingen; Universitäts-Bibliothek, Königsberg; Herzogliche Bibliothek, Meiningen; Königliche Öffentliche Bibliothek, Stuttgart; Bibliothek des stenograph-ischen Gymnasiastenvereins nach Stolze, Zeitz; and the collections of C.E.B. (Havette coll.) and W.J.C.

Another edition with the title "Nouvelle Methode", etc., is dated 1691. Copies are in the Sächsische Landesbibliothek, Dresden; S.L.D.; and Universitäts-Bibliothek, Göttingen.

Another edition with the same title, dated 1692, is in the Bibliothek des stenographischen Gymnasiastenvereins nach Stolze, Zeitz.

Another edition with the same title, dated 1693, is in the Bibliothek des stenographischen Gymnasiastenvereins nach Stolze, Zeitz; and the collection of C.E.B. (Havette coll.).

The full titles and bibliographical descriptions of the French editions are given in René Havette's *Bibliographie de la Sténographie française*, Paris, 1906, pp. 169–173.

Many later editions appeared in German, for particulars of which see Alfred Junge's *Die Vorgeschichte der Stenographie in Deutschland*, Leipzig, 1890, pp. 71–110, and the same author's "Dokumente zur älteren Steno-graphiegeschichte Deutschlands" in *Archiv für Stenographie*, Berlin, Jahrg. xlvi, pp. 18–25 (1894).

CHARLES ALOYS RAMSAY (fl. 1670–1680), who has been aptly dubbed the knight-errant of stenography, describes himself as "Nobilis Scoti". It has been suggested that he was a son of Charles Ramsay, who lived in Prussia in the seventeenth century, became town councillor of Elbing, and died there in 1669 (K. Faulmann's *Historische Grammatik der Stenographie*, 1887, p. 185). Historians of Elbing, however, though mentioning many members of this old Scottish family, are silent concerning the author of "Tacheographia", whose connection with the Ramsays of Elbing has not been established. He has sometimes been confused with the Chevalier Andrew Michael Ramsay (1686–1743), author of "Les Voyages de Cyrus" (cf. *Biographia Britannica*, 2nd ed., vol. 1, p. 536).

Ramsay seems to have spent the greater part of his life in Germany, but his travels took him into France and Italy. He was at Frankfort-on-the-Maine in 1677, when he wrote the preface to his Latin translation of a treatise on chemistry, "Utiles Observationes", originally written in German by Johann Kunckel, Baron von Loewenstern. The preface is signed "Dabam Francofurti ad Mœnum, ipsis nundinis autumnalibus. Anno 1677. Viri Illustrissimi Vestrique Studiosissimo Favete Carolo Aloysio Ramsaio." The book was dedicated to the Royal Society and published in 1678 at London and Rotterdam. Ramsay exalts the importance of chemistry and praises the society. He refers to the king of England as "nostrum regem", and his allegiance to that monarch is implied in the sentence: "ego, qui unum vobiscum eundemque Regem ac Dominum colo et veneror".

His shorthand treatise appeared originally at Frankfort, in Latin and German, in the second half of 1678. Although some posthumous editions of Ramsay's book are described as "aus den Englischen ins Teutsche übersetzet", no edition in English is known. The reason is clear from the preface to his "New vermehrte Tacheographia", dated Leipzig, 2 January 1679, which throws an interesting light on the circumstances which led him to undertake the work:

"Although the swift writers were praised by Cicero, such a system of rapid writing is, so far as I am aware, little known at the present time, with the exception of certain studious and curious persons in England, who take down sermons in church word for word very easily and swiftly. Thus I have known a noble Englishman at Messina in Sicily who was an expert in this science, and yet another who travelled with me a few years ago from Rome to Marseilles in France. And although this way of writing is well known to me, I have observed that it is applied only to the English language. For this reason I have tried to find out how other languages, especially those which are now most commonly used, could be as easily and rapidly written. I began some months ago with the Latin tongue, which is very widely known and used by nearly all the nations of Europe."

In the winter of 1680 Ramsay appears to have been in Paris, his address being given as "rue Dauphine, au bout du Pont-neuf, à l'Image S. Pierre, chez un Bourelier". The French translation of his shorthand manual by A. D. G. published in that year contained a long and fulsome dedication to Louis XIV, "le seul Roy qui a mérité de porter les noms glorieux de Grand et de Bon". The author's preface is dated Paris, 9 December 1680, and he prints an extract from the royal privilege which he had secured from Louis on 19 December, granting him the exclusive right to publish and sell his shorthand for a period of ten years, infringement being punishable by a fine of 3000 livres and confiscation of the offending books.

(Alfred Junge's *Die Vorgeschichte der Stenographie in Deutschland*, Leipzig, 1890, pp. 61–110; R. Havette's *Bibliographie de la Sténographie française*, Paris, 1906, pp. 171–3; T. A. Fischer's *The Scots in Germany*, Edinburgh, 1902, p. 233; J. Ferguson's *Bibliotheca Chemica*, Glasgow, 1906, II, 243–4; *Allgemeine Deutsche Biographie*, Band 53, Leipzig, 1907, pp. 194–5.)

A comparison of Ramsay's German "Tacheographia" with Shelton's "Tachygraphy" (see pp. 42–3) leaves little room for doubt that the latter work formed the basis of Ramsay's system. The two alphabets are identical, with the exception of the characters for *h* and *w*, the method of vocalisation is the same in both, and there are other points of resemblance. Although Shelton's name is nowhere mentioned by Ramsay, the accusation of plagiarism brought against the latter by Fossé (*Cours théorique et pratique de sténographie*, Paris, 1829, p. 62) can hardly be justified in view of Ramsay's explicit declaration that his object was to adapt to other languages an art hitherto applied only to English (*New vermehrte Tacheographia*, Vorrede). He accordingly introduced such modifications as he considered necessary to suit the peculiarities of the German language, reducing considerably the number of double and treble consonants as well as the signs for prefixes and suffixes, whilst he provided special symbols for *ch*, *sh* (*sch*), *st* and *th*. The French version shows even greater divergencies from the original, several of Shelton's alphabetic characters being discarded in favour of simpler and more facile signs. The fullest descriptions of Ramsay's system will be found in A. Junge's *Die Vorgeschichte der Stenographie in Deutschland*, 1890, pp. 97–108, and O. W. Melin's *Stenografiens Historia*, II, 16–18, 1929.

Thoographia, | or, | A New Art | of | Short-Hand. | Being | A more Natural, Grammatical, | and easie Method than any yet | Extant. | Originally Invented by | Abraham Nicholas, M.A. | Enlarged and Published by *Thomas Slater:* | And approved of by the Ablest Pen-Men | in *London.* | Licensed April 1. 1692. R. Midgley. | *London,* | Printed and Sold by *Henry Mortlock* at the Sign of | the *Phenix* in St. *Pauls Church-yard,* and at his | Shop in *Westminster-Hall,* *W. Freeman* at the Bi- | ble over against the *Middle Temple-Gate* in *Fleet-* | *street.* *S. Manship* at the *Black Bull* in *Cornhil,* | and *J. Garret* at the South-side of the *Royal-Ex-* | *change* in *Cornhil,* 1692.

[402⁴.]

6 × 3¾ in., 8vo, pp. (20)+40+15 engraved plates (numbered 1 to 15), and engraved title-page and dedication printed on one side. No headlines to pages. Ornamental initial letters to each chapter. Sign. A–D4 in eights. The engraved title, which is surrounded by calligraphical figures and flourishes, reads as follows:

ΘΟΟΓΡΑΦΙΑ | μᾶλλον ἀὲι | ΘΟΟΓΕΓΡΑΦΥΙΑ | και γραματικῶς | συνεϚ αλμένη | Sive | *Ars nova Thoogra-* | *phiæ Inventa ab* | *Abr*: *Nicholas.* | M.A. | *Sculpta vero & aucta à* | *Thoma Slater.*

Leaves 1ᵃ–2ᵇ blank, 3ᵃ "Ehmamp censori", 3ᵇ "Liber lectori", 4ᵃ "Advertisement", 4ᵇ blank, 5ᵃ Engraved title, 5ᵇ blank, 6ᵃ Letterpress title, 6ᵇ blank, 7ᵃ Engraved dedication in Latin, 7ᵇ blank, 8ᵃ–8ᵇ "The Publisher to the Reader...Thomas Slater, July 12. 1692", 9ᵃ–12ᵇ "The Author's Preface to his Intended (though then unfinished) Work", 13ᵃ–13ᵇ Address to the Reader signed "John Ayres, April 30. 1692", 14ᵃ Latin verses by R. Ainsworth, 14ᵇ Recommendation signed by six writing masters, 15ᵃ–15ᵇ "A New Art of Short-Hand", 16ᵃ Engraved plate of alphabet, 16ᵇ blank, 17ᵃ–17ᵇ Text,. 18ᵃ Engraved plate of vowels' places, etc., 18ᵇ–19ᵃ blank, 19ᵇ–20ᵃ Engraved plate of prepositions, 20ᵇ blank, 21ᵃ–22ᵇ Text, 23ᵃ blank, 23ᵇ Engraved plate of the initial characters, 24ᵃ–29ᵇ Text, 30ᵃ Engraved plate of pronouns, auxiliary verbs, etc., 30^b blank, 31^a–33^b Text, 34^a blank, 34^b–35^a Engraved plates of contractions, 35^b blank, 36^a–37^b Text, 38^a blank, 38^b–39^a Engraved plates of contractions, 39^b blank, 40^a–41^b Text, 42^a blank, 42^b–43^a Engraved plates of contractions, 43^b blank, 44^a–44^b Text, 45^a blank, 45^b–46^a Engraved plates of contractions, 46^b blank, 47^a–47^b Text, 48^a blank, 48^b Engraved plate of contractions, Lord's Prayer and Creed, etc., in shorthand, 49^a–49^b Text Finis, 50^a–53^b blank.

The first edition of Nicholas's "Thoographia" was entered on the Stationers' Register to H. Mortlock on 26 July 1692 (Roxb. *Transcript*, III, 406), and was announced in the Term Catalogue, Michaelmas 1692 (*T.C.* II, 427). Copies are in B.M.L. (7942.aa.36 and 7942.aa.42 (wanting engraved title-page and dedication)); C.L.M. (Byrom coll., 2.k.3.54); N.L.S. (Warden coll., Wn.852, wanting engraved title-page); Queens' College Library, Cambridge; L.C.W. (Z56.N59, William Blair's copy with his MS. note dated 1808: "The only copy I have ever seen"); L.N.Y. (Beale coll., Reserve, wanting engraved title-page and 1 plate); P.L.L. (O'Donnell coll., wanting engraved title-page and dedication); and W.J.C. A copy was in C.L.W.

A second edition was issued with the following imprint: "London: printed and sold by Henry Mortlock at the Sign of the Phoenix in St. Paul's Church-yard, and W. Freeman at the Bible over against the Middle Temple-Gate in Fleetstreet, 1697." The only recorded copy is in L.N.Y. (Beale coll., *IDS p.v.12, no. 2).

No copy of the third edition has been located.

The fourth edition has the imprint: "London: printed for William Davis, at the Black-Bull, over against the Royal-Exchange in Cornhill. 1699." The only recorded copy is in L.N.Y. (Howard coll., Reserve).

Nicholas was one of the first to perceive, what so many of the early system makers failed to realise, that the true aim of shorthand is "not to write much in a little room, but much in a little time". He pointed out, as Shelton and Coles had done, that the "knacky contractions" for long sentences so much in favour with Rich and his imitators were really a hindrance to rapid writing since the stenographer must perforce wait until the last word of the sentence had been uttered before he could write the corresponding symbol, while the variation of a single word in the sentence must cause mental hesitation and so retard speed. He concludes that "the speaker ought to be followed word by word (if possible)", and that "a word should no sooner fall from his mouth but it should be transubstantiated into ink". Unfortunately, Nicholas's alphabet was as ill-chosen as those of most of his predecessors, and his method of vocalisation was equally inadequate. In writing the pronouns and auxiliary verbs he had recourse to the expedient, already adopted by Mason and Coles, of differentiating them by their position in relation to a real or imaginary line. He advocated the writing of each word separately in order to secure greater legibility.

ABRAHAM NICHOLAS (d. about 1690) must have been living in 1684, as he quotes in the preface to his "Thoographia" from William Addy's "Stenographia", first published in that year (see p. 104). He calls Addy "Mr. A. Y." Nicholas was already in his grave, however, when his work was published in 1692 by Thomas Slater, and biographical particulars are lacking. It has been conjectured that he was the father of Abraham Nicholas, schoolmaster near St Mary Magdalen's, Southwark, whose name appears in "Thoographia" as one to whom would-be learners of the system could apply for instruction in the art. In his "List of Surviving Maister-Pen-Men", 1699, Pepys includes a "Nicholas, pupil of Mr. Story, Maister of yᵉ Free School at Sᵗ Mary Magdalene's, Southwark". The schoolmaster is perhaps identical with "that Ingenious Penman Mʳ Abraham Nicholas Junʳ in Cushion Court in Broad Street" to whom George Bickham dedicated his "Alphabets in all the Hands of Great Britain", and who was probably the author of "The Young Accomptant's Debitor and Creditor; or an Introduction to Merchants' Accounts, after the Italian Manner", published in 1711. Nicholas claims to have conceived the idea of his shorthand ten years before his book was written and to have "searched all the Printed Authors" that he could light upon who had treated of the subject.

Another Abraham Nicholas, a son of the schoolmaster, was born in 1692. He was a writing master with his father at the Hand and Pen in Cushion Court, near Austin Friars, Broad Street, whence, according to Massey, he published "The Young Penman's Copy Book" engraved by Bickham in 1715. Shortly

123

after this Nicholas moved his school to Clapham. In 1719 he issued "The Penman's Assistant and Youth's Instructor", and in 1722 his most important work entitled "The Compleat Writing Master", with the author's portrait and 32 plates engraved by Bickham. Soon afterwards, having handed over the school to his brother James, Abraham Nicholas went abroad and is said by Massey to have died about 1744.

James Nicholas was still in charge of the school at Clapham in 1763.

(*D.N.B.*; Sir Ambrose Heal's *The English Writing Masters and their Copy Books*, 1931, pp. 78–80; William Massey's *The Origin and Progress of Letters*, 1763, pp. 109–111.)

INDEX TO AUTHORS

Lightning Source UK Ltd.
Milton Keynes UK
UKHW010745060819
347479UK00001B/82/P